Developing Talent and Managing People in the Family Enterprise

Editor
Rhian-Anwen Hamill

Managing director
Sian O'Neill

Developing Talent and Managing People in the Family Enterprise
is published by

Globe Law and Business Ltd
3 Mylor Close
Horsell
Woking
Surrey GU21 4DD
United Kingdom
Tel: +44 20 3745 4770
www.globelawandbusiness.com

Developing Talent and Managing People in the Family Enterprise

ISBN 9781837231492
EPUB ISBN 9781837231508
Adobe PDF ISBN 9781837231515

Table of contents

Introduction 5
Rhian-Anwen Hamill
RAH Partners

I. **The psychology of inheritance: behaviour, family dynamics and the challenge of wealth transfer** 9
Greg B Davies
Oxford Risk
Sonya Gladstone
Rhian-Anwen Hamill
RAH Partners

II. **Next-generation talent: practical pathways for developing future leaders in business families** 27
Jennifer East
ONIDA Family Advisors

III. **Beyond the inheritor: addressing the family system in next-generation education** 45
Jessica McGawley
Dallington
Sonya Gladstone
Rhian-Anwen Hamill
RAH Partners

IV. **What high-performance sport can teach families: leadership, teamwork and individual talent** 57
Colby Richardson
Blue Forge Capital
Sonya Gladstone
Rhian-Anwen Hamill
RAH Partners

V. **Family matters: advising families on reputation and privacy in the age of AI** 73
James Hann
Digitalis

VI. **Why investment decisions are not only about money: navigating goals and building family consensus** 87
Maya Prabhu
J.P. Morgan Private Bank
Sonya Gladstone
Rhian-Anwen Hamill
RAH Partners

VII. **Investment best practice in family offices** 101
Samuel Lawson
Samuel Shaw
Sally Tennant
Acorn Capital Advisers

VIII. **Preserving the family voice: legal insights into governance and generational wealth** 121
Suzanne Johnston
Stephenson Harwood LLP

About the authors 138

About Globe Law and Business 144

Introduction

Rhian-Anwen Hamill
RAH Partners

It is with great pleasure that I have gathered this group of talented colleagues for this special report: *Developing Talent and Managing People in the Family Enterprise*. Several of the authors are professional friends with whom I have collaborated for several decades; others are more recent partners in my network of family advisers. All speak from a place of expertise, whether as consultants, senior advisers or family members themselves.

People are an organisation's most valuable asset, and this is no less true in a privately owned enterprise. But the time spent on managing tangible assets (eg, portfolio performance or trust structures) dwarfs the time and effort given to the intangible assets – human capital – and the sometimes complicated dynamics surrounding businesses and capital. The interplay between family members, advisers and executives creates a unique backdrop of complexity. This report aims to shed light on these matters and offers insights into what is required to sustain wealth, harmony and a legacy.

The chapter co-authored with behavioural finance expert Greg B Davies discusses transition. Thanks to the impending 'Great Wealth Transfer', we are entering an era of unprecedented transition, with trillions in assets being passed to the next generation. This chapter reminds us that inheritance involves a delicate mixture of grief, identity and responsibility; it is rarely just about money. Being forearmed is vital and effective communication is the first step in moving from a risk of regret to a state of readiness. This concept of 'readiness' also features in Jennifer East's intelligent and practical chapter on developing the next generation. She explains that many families wait for readiness to arrive, as if it were a birthday, whereas in reality, readiness must be built very intentionally. This necessitates a move from *ad hoc*, informal engagement to creating 'lived learning' environments where the next generation can practise safely, with guidance, before they are required to make significant decisions.

The chapter co-authored with Jessica McGawley, a respected psychologist working with families of wealth, demonstrates how we cannot prepare the next generation without also preparing the current one. When family patterns and historical dynamics are left unexplored, they can manifest unhelpfully elsewhere. Parents must 'switch hats' from business leaders to emotional supporters so that the family can function as a cohesive cohort.

To add spice to the mix, the similarities between high-performance family businesses and the world of elite sport are considered in the chapter co-authored with Colby Richardson and Sonya Gladstone which draws on their backgrounds in competitive rowing. Team sports demand a unity of purpose, a balance of internal rivalry with outward collaboration and a commitment to meritocracy. Sound familiar? A family business is, in many ways, just like a high-performance team – it benefits from the same rigour in coaching and feedback that one would find in a gold medal-winning crew!

Looking to the future, James Hann of Digitalis highlights a 'new normal' in which the traditional advice to 'stay hidden' is no longer viable. In the age of large language models and artificial intelligence, a vacuum of information is quickly filled by algorithms that prioritise relevance over veracity. For the modern family, protecting a reputation now requires a proactive stance, shaping the digital footprint rather than just seeking to erase it.

The next two chapters turn to financial matters directly. First, in the chapter co-authored with the supremely experienced Maya Prabhu of J.P. Morgan, the core question that must precede any allocation of capital is posed: "What is the wealth for?" Without a consensus on the purpose of wealth – whether it is a safety net, a tool for social impact or a driver for growth – conflict is inevitable. Once that purpose is defined, the 'investment engine' can be built to support it. Acorn Capital Advisers' Samuel Lawson, Samuel Shaw and Sally Tennant – who have many decades of leadership in this field under their belts – then provide insight on investment best practice, noting that the chief investment officers of the most successful family offices need not only market skills, but also the diplomacy and emotional intelligence required to navigate family politics.

Finally, Suzanne Johnston of Stephenson Harwood provides a terrifically eloquent reminder in her chapter that family constitutions must be more than dry legal templates; they must capture the "wit, warmth and vision" of the family. A family lawyer's role here is to be the expert listener, ensuring that the legal frameworks are harmonised with the family's authentic voice.

The experts who have contributed to this report have come together to share their insights at a time of rapid technological and social change. I am hugely grateful to them all, and my sincere thanks go especially to Sonya Gladstone, my colleague who has worked closely with me on every aspect of this project, and whose support is very much appreciated. Whether you are a family member navigating your own succession or an adviser seeking to better serve your clients, we hope that the message is clear: pay heed to human elements. By investing in the people, the processes and the 'behavioural infrastructure' of the family enterprise, you will ensure that wealth is not just preserved but given the meaning and purpose that it needs to thrive across generations.

While inheritance is often treated as a legal or financial event, the passing of a property title or a financial portfolio is, in truth, one of the most emotionally complex transitions that a family can encounter.

I. The psychology of inheritance: behaviour, family dynamics and the challenge of wealth transfer

Greg B Davies
Oxford Risk
Sonya Gladstone
Rhian-Anwen Hamill
RAH Partners

1. Introduction: why inheritance is rarely just about money

We are entering an era of unprecedented transition. Economists have termed this the 'Great Wealth Transfer' – a seismic shift that will see trillions in assets pass from the current wealth-holding generation to their successors. With projections estimating the transfer of approximately $80 trillion in the United States and £5.5 trillion in the United Kingdom by 2050, the rising generation is poised to become the wealthiest cohort in history.[1] This shift is not merely a statistical curiosity; it makes conversations around transition and succession more vital than ever before.

While inheritance is often treated as a legal or financial event, the passing of a property title or a financial portfolio is, in truth, one of the most emotionally complex transitions that a family can encounter.[2] We contend that inheritance is the point where grief, identity and responsibility collide. Decisions are frequently made under the heavy weight of emotional strain and uncertainty, deeply entangled with the memories and values that form a family's and an individual's financial identity. Understanding that inheritance is about far more than the movement of assets is central to the work of providing meaningful counsel.

In this chapter, we argue that the primary challenges of inheritance arise not from a lack of intelligence, but from predictable human behaviours – challenges that are amplified when decisions must be made collectively, across individuals with different preferences, perspectives and levels of influence. To explore this, we have come together to discuss the human dynamics behind the transfer of wealth and to offer a way of thinking about – and designing for – these challenges.

First, we examine why inheritance is psychologically so demanding, exploring the roles of regret, inertia and the 'power of the starting point'. We address the 'crisis of clarity' within families, investigating why even the best-intentioned parents and heirs often fail to communicate effectively.

Second, we analyse the pitfalls of collective decision making. We discuss how families often underestimate the genuine differences between family members, how authority and perceived seniority can suppress other vital views and why the underlying decision structure is often the hidden cause of failure.

Finally, we explore the complex themes of control and legacy – the 'King Lear' problem – and offer family constitutions as a form of essential behavioural infrastructure. We consider the nuances of timing, skipped generations and the unique position of surviving spouses, emphasising the need to understand individual financial personalities within the broader family context.

In conclusion, we suggest how to shift awareness and focus from the risk of regret to readiness. By prioritising the human capital behind a transition, we aim to provide a clear picture of what 'good' looks like: an inheritance process accomplished with skill and care, and with the recognition that wealth transfer is ultimately about people, relationships and decisions families can live with.

2. The human side of inheritance

2.1 Why inheritance is so hard

Inheritance involves a unique confluence of challenging contexts that makes it particularly difficult to navigate. Frequently, there is a profound emotional load tethered to the transition, as the financial process often intersects with the stages of bereavement and other dynamics. In many cases, inheritance can become a lightning rod for the anger phase of grief: the distribution of assets provides a target for the negative emotions that family members may be experiencing, often creating rifts between members at an already sensitive time. Whether it is the bereavement, the quiet guilt at distributive decisions or an intense, often burdensome sense of obligation to uphold a legacy that one did not create, wealth carries an emotional weight that far exceeds its numerical value.

Perhaps most challenging is that inheritance often serves as the first explicit acknowledgement of dormant sibling dynamics. Longstanding narratives of rivalry, perceived favouritism or historical roles re-emerge with new intensity, creating undercurrents that are exacerbated by the fact that behaviour is driven as much by the *perceived fairness* of the process as by the objective financial outcomes.

When these dynamics collide, they often trigger a spiral of negative emotion and subsequent inertia. The evidence of this struggle is stark: research by Capital Group reveals that 60% of inheritors regret how they managed their transition, with one-third specifically regretting a failure to invest more proactively.[3] While the outside world may view the recipient as the fortunate beneficiary of a 'gift', the internal reality is often one of profound complexity and isolation.

These outcomes are rarely the result of a simple absence of logic; rather, they reflect decisions shaped by a constellation of behavioural mechanisms, in which the need for emotional comfort often

Perhaps most challenging is that inheritance often serves as the first explicit acknowledgement of dormant sibling dynamics.

outweighs longer-term considerations. Among the most prominent patterns observed in inheritance contexts are:

- 'status quo bias'[4] – the tendency to stick with what one already has rather than initiate change;
- the 'endowment effect',[5] whereby assets acquire additional emotional value simply because they are owned; and
- 'decision paralysis',[6] where choices are deferred or avoided altogether when the stakes feel high or the consequences irreversible.

These mechanisms do not operate in isolation; nor do they represent an exhaustive list. Rather, they interact and reinforce one another, creating powerful behavioural headwinds at precisely the moments when clear, deliberate decisions are most needed.

When these mechanisms converge, emotional comfort becomes the binding constraint on decision making. Inherited wealth is subsequently managed to protect the individual's immediate psychological safety rather than to serve their long-term purpose. When we step back to examine these factors, it becomes clear why inheritance is so complex and why addressing the human element is the only way to move from paralysis towards a thriving, purposeful legacy.

2.2 Regret, inertia and why starting points matter

Once these behavioural forces are in play, the question becomes not whether regret will arise, but how it will manifest. In the context of wealth transition, regret more often stems from inaction than from poor action. This reflects a well-established finding in the behavioural psychology of regret: while short-term regret is often associated with actions taken, longer-term and more consequential regrets tend to concern failures to act and missed opportunities.[7] Inheritance decisions, frequently delayed or avoided under emotional strain, therefore create fertile ground for this pattern of regret.

In practice, this most often appears as inertia. Inheritors allow significant capital to sit idle or retain inherited portfolios by default mistaking stasis for prudence. The familiar feels safe; the effort of deciding feels risky. What results is not a considered long-term strategy, but the quiet continuation of whatever state happens to exist at the moment of transfer.

The importance of the starting point becomes particularly clear when we consider two inheritors who receive exactly the same inheritance consisting of the same portfolio of assets of identical economic value. In one case, the portfolio is encashed *before* it is passed on and the

In the context of wealth transition, regret more often stems from inaction than from poor action.

inheritor receives the value in cash. In the other, the portfolio is transferred *as is* and the inheritor receives the assets directly. From a purely financial perspective, these situations are equivalent. Behaviourally, they are often very different.

Where assets are received directly, the portfolio becomes the default. It carries emotional weight and can persist unchanged for long periods, even when it no longer reflects the inheritor's needs or circumstances. By contrast, where the same portfolio is encashed prior to transfer, the inheritor faces a different challenge: the need to actively reinvest a large sum of cash. This typically involves a sequence of difficult decisions – about risk, timing and implementation – each of which can be emotionally uncomfortable. In practice, this often leads to delay or partial investment, with the cost of forgone market participation compounding quietly over time.

Where an inherited portfolio is broadly appropriate and not poorly constructed, remaining invested avoids both the emotional strain and the financial drag associated with putting capital back to work. The inheritor continues to participate in markets without having to overcome the psychological hurdles that accompany large, explicit investment decisions.

The central point is not that one starting position is inherently superior, but that starting positions matter. The form in which wealth is received can set individuals on very different behavioural paths, shaping outcomes over years or decades even when the underlying inheritance is identical. It is in these early moments of transition – often unnoticed at the time – that the foundations for either long-term regret or purposeful growth are quietly laid.

2.3 A crisis of clarity, not intent

It is important to note that these observations are made with the aim not of assigning blame, but of understanding why even well-intentioned families so often struggle to achieve clarity. It would be easy to criticise the senior generation for a perceived failure to communicate how to navigate financial transitions or how to cultivate the 'positive inertia' required for success. However, the evidence suggests a much deeper disconnect. Research conducted by Capital Group[8] highlights an illustrative disparity: while 88% of wealth holders believe that they have communicated their plans effectively, only 38% of heirs feel satisfied with the process. This is not a crisis of intent, but a crisis of clarity – one that emerges when families are forced to rely on unstructured communication in situations that demand careful, shared sense-making and is then compounded by familiar psychological barriers.

When inheritance finally forces a collective decision, families are often attempting, for the first time, to resolve deeply emotional issues in a group setting – at precisely the moment at which the psychological stakes are highest.

At the heart of this crisis of clarity is a structural issue that is often overlooked: many families simply lack established forums in which to practise making decisions together. In the absence of such forums, communication defaults to *ad hoc* conversations, bilateral exchanges or assumptions that shared understanding already exists. When inheritance finally forces a collective decision, families are often attempting, for the first time, to resolve deeply emotional issues in a group setting – at precisely the moment at which the psychological stakes are highest.

The first barrier is the simple avoidance of emotionally charged conversations. Families often carry a history of perceived negative outcomes or a general cultural aversion to confrontation. A parent may have witnessed inheritance trigger conflict between themselves and their parents and, consequently, may be reluctant to invite that same negativity into their own family unit. Similarly, memories of sibling rivalry or perceived favouritism in previous generations can lead to a defensive silence. Further, we often see that where wealth holders are the original creators, they have no personal experience of the transition that they are asking their heirs to undergo. Through no fault of their own, they may lack the specific vocabulary required to address such a complex emotional landscape effectively.

Second is the 'illusion of transparency'. Often, wealth holders believe that their intentions are self-evident, operating under the assumption that "they will surely know what I mean". While this is usually well intentioned, rooted in a belief that their children are "smart enough to understand", it can be just as damaging as total avoidance. Intent that is not explicitly articulated is intent that is open to misinterpretation. Finally, many wealth holders fall back on a sense of unfounded optimism, believing that because their heirs are trustworthy and capable, it will simply "all work out".

These behavioural barriers are then amplified by how family decision making is typically structured in practice. Frequently, a family's first attempt at collective decision making occurs in the high-stakes shadow of a wealth transfer – precisely the moment least suited to experimentation, disagreement or emotional discovery. As we have established, inheritance is so heavily loaded with psychological complexity that it is nearly impossible to navigate smoothly if the family has not already 'practised' smaller-scale collaboration.

This leads to the second pitfall: the failure to distinguish family discussions from business boards. Business boards are often, by design, agenda driven, authority aware and decision focused. Family discussions, by contrast, require space for divergence, reflection and the revisiting of issues that may not resolve neatly or quickly. While a

While the concept of fostering group communication may appear straightforward at the outset, the reality is a delicate ecosystem of human dynamics that demands far more intentional design than is often anticipated.

wealth holder is generally comfortable in this environment, family systems require a different approach – and expertise that lies outside the boardroom. They thrive when members reflect together to discuss difficult issues or revisit historical ones, and when they can tolerate a level of ambiguity that may be antithetical to corporate logic. This is where an external adviser can add the most value – not by providing answers, but by designing and facilitating a process through which shared understanding can emerge. A wealth holder may say something once and believe that the task is complete. But saying is not hearing and hearing is not understanding. Shared understanding requires structure, repetition and time.

3. When families decide together – and why it's hard

We have established that inheritance is a mix of emotional, psychological and technical complexities. As we have explored, this journey requires families to navigate deeply embedded histories, identities and behaviours, each of which every family member brings to the table in their own unique way. While the concept of fostering group communication may appear straightforward at the outset, the reality is a delicate ecosystem of human dynamics that demands far more intentional design than is often anticipated.

In this section, we outline two common ways in which families, despite their best intentions, frequently stumble when attempting to resolve this vital issue and the key reminder to take away from each. We then move to our contention that structuring and guiding communications and decisions is central to families navigating the psychology of inheritance successfully. At its core, an inheritance decision is a collective act and should be approached as one. Yet by shifting from the individual to the group, we invite a new and distinct set of behavioural challenges that can compromise even the most well-meaning succession plans.

3.1 Underestimating difference

We often rely on comforting aphorisms such as "the apple does not fall far from the tree" to assume that family members share a naturally aligned approach to inheritance decisions. This assumption is particularly seductive in the context of significant wealth, where families typically share similar financial means and social environments. Yet the reality is that families are far less homogeneous than we anticipate – and people systematically underestimate just how different others' preferences and perspectives really are.

A striking, if light-hearted, illustration of this phenomenon can be found in our collaborative event, "Pour Better Decisions: How Wine-Tasting and Investing Benefit from Each Other."[9] In this setting, we demonstrate the power of individual perception by serving the exact same wine to every person in the room. The conditions are identical: the same vintage, the same temperature and a blind tasting. We then ask the participants to plot the wine on a scale from "Very dry" to "Very sweet". One might expect a cluster of similar responses; yet invariably, the results span the entire scale.

While a wine tasting is a world away from the complexities of succession, it serves as a powerful metaphor for how profoundly individual perception can differ, even under identical conditions. If we cannot reach a consensus on the objective sweetness of a liquid in a glass, how can we expect a family to have an instinctively shared view on far more abstract and high-stakes concepts?

In family wealth, these same diverse perceptions apply to situations with profound consequences: risk appetite, liquidity needs, comfort with spending and legacy priorities. The realisation that even members of the same nuclear family, such as siblings, can hold diametrically opposed views on these pillars is essential. Recognising this divergence is not a sign of family dysfunction; rather, it is the first requirement for productive, shared decision making. We must stop assuming alignment and start actively seeking to understand and appreciate the unique 'tastes' that each member brings to the family's financial table.

3.2 Authority and suppressed views

The second stumbling block arises from the natural influence of authority and seniority within families, even when exercised with the best of intentions. Typically, patriarchs, founders or other senior figures are accustomed to shaping outcomes with a singular will – a habit often mirrored in family conversations just as clearly as in the boardroom. This influence generally manifests in two distinct and largely unconscious ways, both of which compromise the integrity of the family's decision-making process:

- contamination, whereby family members genuinely change their own views when exposed to the opinions of an authority figure, often without fully recognising that this shift has occurred; and
- conformity – a more restrictive mode in which individuals retain their own views but choose not to express them, deferring instead to the dominant voice in the room.

Both modes closely parallel corporate board dynamics and introduce what is colloquially known as the 'HIPPO' problem: where the 'highest-paid person's opinion' becomes the default position for the group, not because it is asserted, but because others adapt or withdraw. In the context of family discussions, while we may not be measuring a formal pay structure, this role invariably falls to the head of the holding generation, who may also be the current or former leader of the family's commercial interests.

Drawing parallels with corporate boards is instructive. Many modern boards now recognise the importance of actively surfacing every voice to avoid the perils of groupthink. Families, by contrast, often lack this discipline; ensuring that all perspectives are heard – regardless of position in the family hierarchy – is essential. To navigate these high-stakes conversations successfully, families must learn to dismantle the HIPPO dynamic, moving away from a culture of quiet deference under the banner of respect towards one of genuine, shared deliberation.

3.3 Designing better family conversations

If differences in individual preferences and the quiet influence of authority are the forces that destabilise family harmony, then decision structure becomes the necessary counterweight. We often find that families resist setting rules around how their discussions happen, fearing that structure will introduce a cold, bureaucratic air into what should be an intimate, organic process. However, the reality is quite the opposite. Many families mistakenly believe that a series of fragmented, bilateral conversations can achieve the same outcome as a collective family discussion, when in fact they may benefit far more from a single, deliberately structured family meeting. In truth, unstructured conversations act as a vacuum that is filled by existing

Many families mistakenly believe that a series of fragmented, bilateral conversations can achieve the same outcome as a collective family discussion, when in fact they may benefit far more from a single, deliberately structured family meeting.

power dynamics. Without a clear framework for engagement, the loudest voice or the most established narrative will naturally prevail, stifling the very 'human element' that families are so keen to protect.

To navigate this, families can adopt simple yet profound communication techniques that protect the integrity of every individual perspective. The most effective of these is the discipline of surfacing individual views *prior* to group discussion. By asking family members to articulate their own priorities or risk tolerances in isolation, perhaps through a thinking round around the table or a private reflection, we can separate the formation of an opinion from the social pressure of group deliberation. This ensures that when the family does come together to discuss, the starting point is authentic views rather than an immediate, contaminated consensus.

Furthermore, once the discussion begins, the order of engagement is important. A powerful technique used to dismantle the HIPPO effect is the practice of inviting the least senior or least vocal members to speak first. This prevents the senior generation from inadvertently setting the tone and allows for a democratic exploration of the family's objectives. Quieter introverts are often very thoughtful and their contributions can be valuable when encouraged in this way.

Ultimately, we must understand that communication tools and guidelines are not an end; nor are they strict processes for the purpose of being bureaucratic. Rather, these communication techniques serve as a vital behavioural enabler. Using them can begin to create a 'safe container' in which shared understanding can occur. By intentionally designing the way that they communicate and discuss, families can move beyond the surface-level agreement of the boardroom towards a purposeful, values-led consensus that is resilient enough to last for generations.

4. Designing for legacy – governance, control and alignment

If the internal landscape of a family is defined by its undercurrents and psychological biases, then any external framework – including governance, timing and legal structures – must be designed to support, rather than override, that human reality. Having explored the 'why' of miscommunication, we must now turn our attention to the 'how' of enduring legacy.

In this section, we examine the formal mechanisms that allow a family to move beyond individual intent towards a collective, structured reality. We move from the theoretical to the practical, exploring how a strong behavioural infrastructure can protect the family system from the timeless pitfalls of power, transition and the inevitable divergence of individual financial personalities.

4.1 Control, legacy and the 'King Lear' problem

In the theatre of wealth transition, Shakespeare's *King Lear* remains the ultimate behavioural parable of inheritance. It is a cautionary tale not only of lost power, but also of the psychological fallout that occurs when the structural transfer of assets is used as a proxy for emotional validation and as a substitute for the gradual and inevitable loss of control and influence.

As Shakespeare recognised, passing on assets does not mean passing on control. Once wealth leaves your hands, so should the ability to control or even influence its use. Yet many wealth holders fall into the trap of the 'illusion of control': the belief that they can dictate the behaviour of children, even from beyond the grave. This can lead to a profound sense of betrayal, echoing Lear's lament: "How sharper than a serpent's tooth it is / To have a thankless child."[10] Through a behavioural lens, we might reframe this not as a moral failure of the next generation, but as a systemic failure of misaligned expectations.

This tension typically manifests in two opposing errors. The first is over-control: the attempt to dictate behaviour through restrictions. The second, and perhaps more subtle, is under-use, where an inheritor preserves assets out of respect for the predecessor's memory, even at significant personal cost. These errors can then give rise to regret in the inheritor – an unintended but commonly observed emotional outcome, as discussed earlier.

Lear's eventual realisation that "I did her wrong"[11] serves as a reminder that regret usually arrives only when the damage to the family ecosystem is irreversible. The behavioural case for a successful legacy, therefore, is found not in more rules, but in better processes. The goal is to shape understanding and shared values while the wealth holder is still alive, moving away from a desire to control the outcome towards a commitment to empowering the successor. By shifting the focus from "Who loves us most?" to a shared understanding of process, families can avoid the tragedy of the 'serpent's tooth' and ensure that their wealth serves as a purposeful foundation for the generations to follow.

4.2 Family constitutions as behavioural infrastructure

If part of the tragedy of *King Lear* is the result of misaligned expectations, then we propose the family constitution as a remedy. However, first it is important to clarify what a family constitution is and, perhaps more importantly, what it is not. A family constitution is not a legal instrument designed for the courtroom; nor is it governance theatre – a glossy document intended for show but

The goal is to shape understanding and shared values while the wealth holder is still alive, moving away from a desire to control the outcome towards a commitment to empowering the successor.

of no practical use. Rather, it is a coordination tool designed to shape behaviour. Its value lies not in enforcing compliance, but in setting expectations before stress, hierarchy and emotion distort decision making.

It is important to recognise a common pitfall: when family constitutions are drafted as if they were corporate or business documents, they tend to reproduce the very boardroom dynamics that undermine effective family decision making. Language that is overly formal and rules that are too rigid fail to engage with the human system that the document is meant to support, limiting its behavioural effectiveness.

What works behaviourally is to position the constitution as a coordination tool. Its purpose is to surface the unspoken assumptions that each family member carries and to provide a shared reference point for future decisions. By documenting principles and expectations in advance, families reduce ambiguity and are better able to navigate difficult decisions without having to negotiate values in the heat of a crisis.

There is a parallel here with the 'investing constitution' that one might advocate for individuals. Just as an investor needs decision rules and

Historically, wealth transfer for the recipient was a mid-life event; today, it is increasingly a late-life one. This structural shift introduces a new layer of complexity: by the time an inheritance arrives, the primary inheritors are often already financially independent and established.

emotional guardrails to protect them from their own biases during market volatility, a family needs a constitution to protect its collective legacy from the volatility of group dynamics.

Ultimately, the act of writing these agreements down matters a great deal. Human memory is unreliable and we often edit past conversations through our own differing perceptions. A written constitution protects relationships just as much as it protects capital. It ensures that the family's story is told with all the pages intact, providing a clear, documented foundation. In this light, the constitution is not a restrictive set of rules, but a framework that allows a family to move forward with a shared sense of purpose.

4.3 Timing, skipped generations and longevity

We have seen a structural shift in the way that inheritance is taking place more recently and this is an important shift to address. Historically, wealth transfer for the recipient was a mid-life event; today, it is increasingly a late-life one. This structural shift introduces a new layer of complexity: by the time an inheritance arrives, the primary inheritors are often already financially independent and established. Consequently, we are seeing more transfers that bypass the immediate next generation, with capital moving directly to grandchildren.

While this may be tax efficient, it creates three-generation complexity and communication challenges. Navigating the needs, risk appetites and financial personalities of grandparents, parents and grandchildren simultaneously requires a level of coordination that is higher than what may have worked for families in the past. The potential for friction is high when the generation in the middle is bypassed or tasked with stewarding wealth that they may feel they do not technically own.

Another dimension of longevity is that wealth may pass to a surviving spouse first. In many older cohorts, these spouses may have been under-involved in the granular management of family finances. This responsibility, particularly in the wake of grief, can be associated with specific behavioural responses: lower confidence, high liquidity preference and an emotional attachment to specific assets that the partner may have favoured or a legacy asset that holds particular sentimental value. These responses can mirror the decision paralysis described earlier for inheritors – an urge to preserve capital at all costs, even when doing so fails to meet their own long-term needs. Once again, this is not a failure of intellect, but a natural response.

However, a clear caveat must be noted: these are average tendencies, not absolute rules. There are many surviving spouses who are sophisticated, proactive investors, just as there are grandchildren who are the same. These shifts reinforce the central thesis of our approach: you cannot manage a family based on broad categories. Success in these complex, multilayered transitions requires a deep, individualised understanding of each person's unique financial personality. Only by seeing the individuals behind the roles of spouse, child or grandchild can we build a transition plan that is sufficiently resilient to survive the passage of time.

4.4 Financial personality in a family context

The ultimate goal of any framework is to make explicit what is otherwise implicit. Throughout this chapter, we have explored how families can stumble over misaligned expectations and the illusion of transparency. The remedy lies in moving beyond demographic assumptions – which, as we have seen, almost always fail – towards a more nuanced understanding of individual financial personality.

Some of the most relevant financial personality traits in this context include the following:

- ***Risk Tolerance:*** A stable trait reflecting an individual's reasoned willingness to accept the possibility of lower long-term outcomes in exchange for a greater chance of higher long-term returns.
- ***Confidence:*** How capable and comfortable an individual feels about their ability to make good financial decisions.
- ***Composure:*** An individual's emotional comfort with the ups and downs of their financial journey and their tendency to remain calm in the face of short-term uncertainty and volatility.
- ***Liquidity Preference:*** The degree to which an individual values having quick access to their assets, even at the expense of potential returns.
- ***Familiarity Preference:*** The extent to which an individual prefers investments and strategies that feel familiar or well understood, often supported by a strong narrative.
- ***Impulsivity and Spending Reluctance:*** These shape how quickly and comfortably individuals act on financial decisions and use their wealth.[12]

In a family context, these traits shape the conditions under which group decision making takes place. In the absence of this language, we tend to see dynamics and biases surface to fill the gap – for example, assumptions such as deeming a sibling's high composure to be recklessness or a parent's low confidence as a desire to be controlling. These are often just different degrees of the above traits in each person. By using structured tools to map these traits, we make these invisible differences visible, replacing labels and resentment with empathy and the ability to make collective decisions.

When a family sits down to discuss their constitution or a major investment, having these profiles understood by the individuals means that the group can change the conversation from conflict to alignment. It allows a patriarch to see that his daughter's hesitation is not a lack of interest, but a lower confidence score that can be bolstered with education. It helps a grandchild to understand that a grandparent's under-use of assets is a high spending reluctance that deserves empathy rather than frustration.

Ultimately, understanding financial personality provides a shared language for the family. It offers a neutral, objective vocabulary that allows members to discuss their differences without triggering the 'King Lear' drama of perceived slights or betrayals. By formalising these insights, families can move from a state of accidental conflict to one of intentional, collective decision making. This increases the likelihood that shared wealth will remain a source of unity and a purposeful foundation for generations to follow, rather than a catalyst for division.

5. Conclusion: from regret to readiness

The Great Wealth Transfer is often discussed as a logistical hurdle for financial and legal professionals. Yet, as we have explored, the true challenge lies in the internal landscape of the family. To navigate this transition successfully, we must fundamentally reframe what 'good' looks like. In the context of inheritance, success is not found in the optimisation of a portfolio or in the control of a legacy from beyond the grave. Rather, success is defined by decisions that people can live with.

This requires a shift towards modest ambition and behavioural realism. We must understand that families are not corporate entities, but emotional ecosystems where the 'modest ambition' of maintaining harmony is often more valuable than the pursuit of technical perfection. Moving from a state of regret to one of readiness is not an overnight transformation; it is the result of early, repeated and supported conversations. It requires structured group processes that protect the least vocal, alongside the integration of behaviourally informed advice. Most importantly, this process requires respect for individual differences, supported by a shared language around individual financial personality.

When we prioritise the human capital behind the transition, we understand that the objective of wealth transfer is not merely the preservation of capital, but the preservation of relationships, the enablement of stewardship and the support of long-term wellbeing. When a transition is accomplished with skill, care and a deep understanding of the individuals involved, wealth can become a purposeful foundation for the next chapter of the family legacy.

Notes

1 Tara Loader Wilkinson, "The Great Wealth Transfer: The Shift of Assets to the Youth", *Savills Portfolio*, https://portfolio.savills.com/insight/the-great-wealth-transfer-the-shift-of-assets-to-the-youth/.

2 Greg B Davies, "The Psychology of Inheritance", *Oxford Risk Blog*, 24 November 2025, www.oxfordrisk.com/blog-posts/the-psychology-of-inheritance.

3 Capital Group, "Lack of Holistic Advice Drives Inheritors to Regret", *Financial Times*, Partner Content, https://capitalgroup.ft.com/lack-of-holistic-advice-drives-inheritors-to-regret.

4 Ziyang Cheng, "The Impact of Status Quo Bias on Peoples Choices", *Advances in Economics, Management and Political Sciences* 10:111–115, September 2023, www.researchgate.net/publication/373896860_The_Impact_of_Status_Quo_Bias_on_Peoples_Choices.

5 Yanjiang Guo, "Unveiling the Endowment Effect: Understanding Its Significance and Applications", *Advances in Economics, Management and Political Sciences* 60:199–205, January 2024, www.researchgate.net/publication/377180071_Unveiling_the_Endowment_Effect_Understanding_Its_Significance_and_Applications.

6 Diana Drake, "5 Truths about Behavioral Economics and Studying Consumer Behavior", *Wharton Global Youth Program*, 1 February 2023, https://globalyouth.wharton.upenn.edu/articles/world-economy/5-truths-about-behavioral-economics-and-studying-consumer-behavior/.

7 T Gilovich and VH Medvec, "The Experience of Regret: What, When, and Why", *Psychological Review*, 102:379–395, 1995, https://psycnet.apa.org/record/1995-24085-001.

8 Capital Group, "Lack of Holistic Advice Drives Inheritors to Regret", *Financial Times*, Partner Content, https://capitalgroup.ft.com/lack-of-holistic-advice-drives-inheritors-to-regret.

9 Greg B Davies, "Pour Better Decisions: How Wine-Tasting and Investing Benefit from Behavioral Science", LinkedIn, 26 October 2024, www.linkedin.com/pulse/pour-better-decisions-how-wine-tasting-investing-benefit-greg-davies-kdrhe/.

10 William Shakespeare, *King Lear*, Act 1, Scene 4, lines 288–289.

11 *Ibid*, Scene 5, line 24.

12 Greg B Davies, "The Role of Financial Personality in Retirement Income Planning", *Oxford Risk Blog*, 15 July 2025, www.oxfordrisk.com/blog-posts/the-role-of-financial-personality-in-retirement-income-planning.

II. Next-generation talent: practical pathways for developing future leaders in business families

Jennifer East
ONIDA Family Advisors

1. Introduction

Families are rightly meticulous about tax, trusts and investment policy. The same discipline is needed for the 'people' work that sustains an enterprise across generations. Drawing on two decades of advising global business families, this chapter sets out a practical approach to developing next-generation talent. It comes amid the largest leadership transition in decades, as younger generations are increasingly seeking meaning and context, while many ownership groups are still developing informally.

A founder once told me that he wanted his children 'ready' before they took a seat; but this readiness never arrived, because it had never been built. The shift was simple but decisive. We began with the individuals – identity, strengths, purpose – before assigning any roles. Readiness subsequently became visible through clear roles and rubrics. Governance forums doubled as classrooms in which judgement was practised, not just decisions recorded. The aim was straightforward: to develop confident owners and future leaders who could hold both purpose and performance, and to help support that journey through a smooth, transparent process.

2. Rethinking readiness

Many families defer involving the next generation until a formal role appears, often saying that they will engage "when they're ready". In practice, readiness does not arrive on inheritance or on a specific birthday; it is developed over time. The families that navigate succession well treat this as a deliberate process, rather than an aspiration. They create time and space for reflection, structured exposure to how decisions are made and guided practice in taking responsibility. Recent interviews with rising-gen leaders and family office executives also underline a preference for practical learning and transparency about the succession process.[1]

Leadership in a family enterprise sits at the intersection of two systems – family and business – with all the visibility, history and emotion that this implies. Classroom learning and short courses can help, but they are insufficient on their own. The capabilities that matter most are practised, not taught, including:

- exercising judgement;
- balancing family and business relationships among stakeholders;
- navigating the tension between legacy and present-future needs;
- weighing trade-offs; and
- contributing constructively to governance.

Leadership in a family enterprise sits at the intersection of two systems – family and business – with all the visibility, history and emotion that this implies. Classroom learning and short courses can help, but they are insufficient on their own.

These capabilities are honed when learning is lived by observing real discussions, preparing for meetings, contributing recommendations and receiving clear feedback on both process and outcome.

Delaying involvement carries costs. Younger family members can feel like guests rather than owners and talented individuals may drift towards careers with little connection to the family's assets or purpose. While an independent career can be an excellent outcome, it must be a conscious choice, planned and supported so that the person still develops as a responsible owner. Either way, families need a thoughtful approach that begins with clarity about purpose and roles and continues with transparent processes for development, assessment and appointment, so that when decisions are made, they are accepted as fair and well grounded. Large-scale survey work also indicates that many family offices engage next-gens informally, while a significant share lack a formal education plan – another reason to move from *ad hoc* to intentional.[2]

It helps to describe readiness plainly. For owners, this requires:

- a sufficient understanding of what the family owns and why;
- a level of financial and business fluency appropriate to the role; and
- the ability to participate in governance by:
    - listening well;
    - asking useful questions; and
    - making decisions in line with agreed principles.

Families that explicitly define role requirements and development steps are less likely to default to personalities or proximity when appointing people

Development should begin before titles change. Age-appropriate exposure, a gradual increase in responsibility and measured authority within clear guardrails enable identity, confidence and judgement to develop in parallel This aligns with good practice in succession planning:

- Start with goals and values;
- Establish transparent processes; and
- Support individuals with structured feedback and coaching so that appointments are based on fit and capability rather than assumption.[3]

3. Identity before role

Families that succeed across generations attend first to the person, then to the position. A next-generation member who has examined values, motivations and strengths is better able to choose whether and how to contribute. This foundation supports resilience under public scrutiny or intra-family disagreement and creates the conditions for voluntary commitment rather than obligation. At the same time look from the top down: define the roles and responsibilities required by the enterprise, then align them with individuals based on demonstrated fit, not convenience or familiarity.

The development methods that support identity are practical and private. Coaching provides a confidential, structured space to test assumptions, clarify purpose and translate values into day-to-day decisions. When a coach works to agreed outcomes with both principal and client, progress becomes visible and relevant to the enterprise. In parallel, mentoring adds lived context through regular touchpoints with a trusted senior who can open networks, share how decisions are made in practice and offer grounded feedback on judgement and tone. In both arrangements, clarity on scope, cadence and confidentiality is essential – the aim is to build capability, not reliance. Alongside individual work, group coaching for siblings or cousins helps each person to understand the strengths and styles of others, so that future collaboration starts on firmer ground.

Identity work begins with self-discovery. Before stepping into any family role, rising leaders will benefit from guided reflection on strengths, leadership style and personal goals. Selective use of objective tools can help them to name patterns and preferences. From there, a simple development plan – encompassing goals, learning experiences, sponsors and milestones – gives shape to growth and a way to mark progress.

Experience then makes identity real. Purposeful assignments (eg, short rotations, project ownership, small-capital collaborations among siblings or cousins, or defined roles in philanthropy) enable younger members to practise judgement and follow-through within clear guardrails and with vital feedback. Meanwhile, peer networks serve as a confidential arena in which to compare notes and normalise the developmental journey.

Sequencing matters. Families that place knowledge before power (eg, through progressive exposure to real discussions, followed by modest mandates) allow individuals' sense of self and judgement to grow together. Early steps might include:

- observing a committee with a short written reflection;
- presenting a brief on a specific decision; or
- taking responsibility for a cross-functional project.

As capability deepens, authority can increase, with clear expectations and feedback at each stage.[4] Common early entry points such as family meetings, observation in owner forums (eg, boards and councils) and philanthropy mirror what rising-gen participants themselves say works best.[5]

4. The owner's competency map

Clarity of identity does not mean channelling everyone into the operating business. In many enterprises, the most durable leadership pathways are plural, with roles including:

- engaged owner;
- family council member;
- trustee or director;
- ambassador for the family purpose; and
- operating executive.

Making these pathways – and the competencies that each requires – explicit reduces the risk of appointments based solely on family relationships and helps younger members to invest in the right skills at the right time.

Each role calls for a different mix of capabilities. A practical competency map for owners typically includes:

- a contextual understanding of what the family owns and why;
- financial and business fluency proportionate to the role;
- an understanding of governance (ie, preparing, listening, asking useful questions and making decisions);
- collaboration across branches and generations; and
- values and ethics as expressed in day-to-day decisions.

Translating these ideas into action requires clear role profiles and rubrics. Role profiles set out purpose, responsibilities, time requirements and expectations for independence. Rubrics describe observable behaviours at ascending levels (eg, baseline, developing, proficient and advanced), so that feedback is specific and comparable. Used consistently, these tools:

- reduce the number of appointments based on subjective factors;
- make expectations clear to candidates; and
- provide a fair basis for selection and review.[6]

Encouragingly, recent survey work indicates that a meaningful minority of family offices now use individual development plans for next-gens which reflect the rubrics described here.[7]

Development then becomes planned rather than improvised. For example, a development plan might start with observing an owner or committee forum through a defined lens such as sustainability, inviting the young family member to identify where risks and opportunities appear. Next, the rising member researches options and drafts a short recommendation on how to integrate that lens into the enterprise's activities. Finally, they lead a pilot to test the proposal within clear guardrails (eg, scope, timing, budget and success measures). Throughout this process, periodic reviews focus on judgement, preparation and contribution – not just outcomes – so that confidence, capability and trust grow together.

When it comes to appointments, applying the same discipline that is expected in senior hiring in family offices helps to preserve trust, with measures including:

- documented criteria tied to the role profile;
- structured interviews and references;
- clear conflict-of-interest rules; and
- a transparent decision process.

Communicating both the criteria and the outcome supports acceptance even when not everyone agrees.[8]

Families also benefit from visible progress. A simple development log or dashboard could include:

- training completed;
- meetings attended;
- contributions made;
- feedback received; and
- next steps agreed.

This allows principals, rising owners and the family office to see movement over time. It also anchors the idea that responsible ownership must be built and refreshed; it is not merely granted by a title or surname.

5. Structures that teach

Governance can be more than a control system. Used well, it becomes a learning tool. Families that treat councils, committees, foundations and project groups as places to practise preparation, discussion and decision making give younger members structured exposure to how owners work together. Clear agendas, pre-reads and defined decision rights make participation purposeful and safe; while linking each forum back to the family's strategy keeps activity from drifting.

Families that treat councils, committees, foundations and project groups as places to practise preparation, discussion and decision making give younger members structured exposure to how owners work together.

Data shows that many families already invite the rising gen into meetings, yet relatively few have structured pathways for this.[9] Design matters – each forum should have:

- a written mandate;
- term limits where appropriate; and
- simple norms for contribution, challenge and confidentiality.

Using role profiles and competency rubrics for committee work helps chairs to set expectations and give specific feedback. Rotating duties such as minute-taking, agenda setting and stakeholder interviews broadens skills and prevents concentration of influence.

As an example, families can turn meetings into practicum moments. For example, a rising member could be assigned to frame one decision with a short options memo, introduce the item and record takeaways for the minutes. Every so often, run a simple mock scenario (eg, a short cash crunch or a key person being unavailable), so that the team can practise decision making safely.[10]

Philanthropy and impact structures offer a particularly useful training ground. Junior boards, thematic giving groups and due diligence projects enable rising members to test values against real choices, see stakeholder effects and learn the discipline of follow-through. When grant making is aligned with the family's stated purpose and includes basic safeguards, it builds judgement and cohesion.[11] This aligns with evidence that purpose-linked forums are among the most common and effective on-ramps for engagement.[12]

Families also benefit from whole-group settings that integrate learning with relationship building. Annual retreats that mix owner education, case discussions and time for history and story help dispersed relatives to build a shared context. Over time, these gatherings normalise participation, make tacit norms visible and create a steady pipeline of prepared contributors for councils, committees and boards.[13] Interviews with families show a shift: they now budget for learning and relationship building, favouring several small touchpoints over a one-off briefing – for example, a couple of site visits and a facilitated dinner over the course of the year.[14]

6. Knowledge before power: making tacit knowhow visible

In most families, what matters most for sound decisions is rarely written down. It lies in habits: how risks are framed, what 'good enough' looks like, when to pause and when to act. Treating this tacit knowhow as something to be taught – before authority is transferred – reduces avoidable errors and anxiety. This is the essence of 'knowledge before power': progressive exposure, practice and feedback that make implicit judgement explicit.[15] Families that start early and emphasise learning-by-doing – including opportunities for failure – report faster gains in confidence and judgement.[16]

A working example

An investment committee was considering whether to exit a legacy holding. Before giving a G3 cousin a vote, the chair asked them to shadow the next two meetings with a focused brief: learn how the group framed downside risk and which thresholds triggered action. Between meetings, the cousin spoke with two members about past exits and drafted a one-page note setting out three choices, the trade-offs for each and a simple 'if/then' timing rule drawn from Carlock and Ward's planning discipline.[17]

At the next session, the cousin introduced the note, listened to the debate and then wrote a two-line entry for the minutes capturing the single factor that tipped the discussion and how their own view evolved. After two practice runs, the cousin used the new rule in relation to a small, low-risk sale and wrote a short note on what they did and how it turned out. That made the 'how we do it' steps clear and built judgement before giving them ongoing authority.

Just as important is capturing the learning so that it travels. Decision logs, short case notes and an 'owner playbook' (eg, setting out principles, thresholds and examples) make judgement portable across branches and over time. Curated repositories – such as a secure owner data room – allow future participants to see how similar calls were made, why and with what results. The goal is simple: reach transition points through shared language and norms that can be accessed and taught consistently, generation after generation.

7. From inheritors' risks to responsible owners

The developmental tasks for wealth creators and those who inherit are not the same. Founders integrate wealth into an already formed identity; inheritors must form identity in the constant presence of wealth, which can result in avoidance, guilt or overcompliance. Spotting these patterns early helps families to design support that is practical and dignified, so that younger members can move from reacting to wealth to using it responsibly.[18]

Capability grows when financial maturity develops alongside knowledge. This involves:

- understanding the sources and uses of capital;
- linking choices to values; and
- setting boundaries and practising generosity and accountability at each stage of life.

Survey data shows that next-gens receive limited education on the subject of money and relationships, even as this becomes more material in adult life.[19]

Joline Godfrey's work on age-appropriate scaffolding is helpful here. For example:

- earlier years could focus on pocket money, with 'spend/save/give' jars and discussion of simple trade-offs;
- adolescence could add using a debit card, budgeting for a school trip and contributing to a phone plan; and
- young adulthood could include filing a tax return with support and taking responsibility for renewing an insurance policy.[20]

Regular, calm conversations about both the mechanics and the meaning of money make these steps easier and reduce secrecy as young adults grow.[21]

Expanding on the real-life mandate for a young adult, families could ask a 21-year-old to run the annual insurance renewal across two properties. This would involve:

- gathering three quotes;
- comparing coverage terms;
- presenting a recommendation;
- executing the choice; and
- writing a short debrief on cost, coverage and lessons learned.

The point is not scale but practice, so that the next generation makes and explains decisions, lives with outcomes and reflects on judgement against agreed principles. Many families still under-resource this work; formal curricula and budgets for learning are often lacking despite clear demand.[22]

Support should be discreet and reliable. Coaching gives individuals a private place to examine assumptions and rehearse choices; while mentoring and peer forums provide lived context and reduce isolation. Over time, this combination shifts the approach from protection to partnership: younger owners learn to bear responsibility with confidence and elders can share authority knowing that knowledge, judgement and character are developing together.[23]

8. Purpose, values and the will to stay together

As money maturity and capability grow, the next task is collective: agreeing why the family stay together as owners. This is a choice, not a default. Families that endure make this choice explicit by agreeing why they should remain aligned – what they want to preserve, develop and create – and by treating purpose as a practical guide for capital, time and attention. In effective ownership groups, purpose sits alongside strategy as a decision filter. It clarifies what the family will do and what it will decline to do; and it gives rising members a reason to participate beyond obligation. Across markets, families are broadening the purpose of wealth beyond performance, with 'purpose of family capital' leading next-gen learning priorities.[24]

For example, one multi-branch family wrote a one-line purpose – "Deploy our patient capital to back enduring enterprises and strengthen our home communities" – and set aside a small annual fund for next gen-led pilots. Cousins proposed options against the stated purpose, presented them at the family council meeting and reported outcomes the following year. Engagement increased because choices were anchored to a shared 'why', not to personalities.[25]

Values must then be made operational. It is not enough to list virtues; values must be reflected in how appointments are made, how risk is framed and how trade-offs are argued and resolved. Helpful tools include:

Process fairness sustains commitment across branches and generations. When participation criteria are transparent, meetings are well run and inclusive, and decisions are communicated with reasons, family members are more likely to accept outcomes even if they disagree.

- a short statement of purpose;
- a family charter that links values to norms of behaviour; and
- simple decision principles (eg, how the family weighs long-term resilience against near-term distributions).

As a practical illustration, if 'stewardship' and 'inclusion' are declared values, the group might adopt long-hold thresholds for investments and reserve speaking time for every branch at key meetings, so that these values are visible in the way in which decisions are made.[26]

Process fairness sustains commitment across branches and generations. When participation criteria are transparent, meetings are well run and inclusive, and decisions are communicated with reasons, family members are more likely to accept outcomes even if they disagree. This sense of procedural justice – "I was heard and I understand why" – is often the difference between grudging compliance and durable support. Jaffe's long-horizon lens on resilient families underscores the value of simple rules, term limits and renewal cadences for roles.[27]

9. The family office as incubator (not just administrator)

A well-run family office can do more than pay bills and consolidate statements; it can promote development by coordinating pathways, people and guardrails. This involves affording exposure (eg, committee observation and project work), arranging mentoring and coaching and aligning reporting so that learning is visible. Done well, the office acts as a quiet integrator, linking opportunities to the competency map and ensuring that each assignment has a sponsor, scope and review. Many offices report expanding services in family engagement and education in recent years, reflecting growing demand and an operational shift towards people development.[28]

For example, one office ran a six-month 'owner apprenticeship' for two cousins. This began with an orientation and observation of an owner forum, with short reflections; they then co-authored a brief for an investment-manager decision; and finally, one led a supplier review while the other coordinated site visits and drafted a one-page update to the foundation's giving guidelines.

The office handled calendars, prep and debriefs; the cousins did the work. By the end, both could point to specific contributions and the board witnessed their judgement in action.

Role clarity is essential. Owner development is not the same as employment. The office can give rising family members context through short projects or internships while basing employment decisions on normal merit processes with clear criteria. This protects standards, avoids subjective appointments and preserves the credibility of both the office and the operating businesses.[29]

Keep support structured without taking over. The office establishes scope, cadence and confidentiality for coaching and mentoring; sets clear boundaries; and provides simple updates and feedback linked to agreed expectations. As judgement grows, authority can be stepped up in stages, with the office stewarding process rather than owning outcomes.[30] The office can also nurture judgement itself: as Andrew Likierman argues, judgement improves with deliberate practice – making many small decisions against clear criteria, followed by brief after-action reviews that capture what was weighed and why.[31]

The office can also host the infrastructure that makes learning portable, including:

- a secure data room for owners (with information on purpose, principles and key policies);
- a calendar of governance and education events; and
- a simple 'owner playbook' of decision norms and examples.

These tools reduce dependence on individual memory, make tacit standards visible and help new participants to arrive ready to contribute.[32]

10. Advisers who develop people (not just plans)

External advisers are most useful when their remit is explicit: to help the family build capability, not dependency. That means setting the developmental agenda upfront – what roles the family needs to fill, what competences must be strengthened and how progress will be assessed. In this way, advice translates into learning rather than languishing in a binder on a shelf. A good engagement letter clarifies scope, decision rights, confidentiality and expected outcomes, aligned to the family's purpose and governance rhythm.[33] This is responsive to a broader gap: many offices still lack documented engagement plans and governance artefacts.[34]

Different roles serve different needs – for example:

- coaches provide a private space to test assumptions and translate values into decisions;
- facilitators design and run meetings so that every voice can contribute and decisions are made cleanly; and
- search partners help to define role profiles, map markets and run disciplined selection.

Keeping these roles distinct avoids confusion and preserves trust – especially when coaching and hiring are happening in parallel.[35]

External advisers are most useful when their remit is explicit: to help the family build capability, not dependency.

One family interested in developing the rising generation engaged a coach for a year to map development plans for three G2 siblings. The remit was clear: agree owner role profiles, set individual learning goals and run quarterly check-ins. In parallel, each sibling was paired with an external mentor aligned to their interests (ie, a foundation chair, a former chief operations officer and an investment professional). The coach handled the process, which comprised two short workshops (values and decision making), a simple plan template and a debrief guide. Mentors provided lived context and opened networks. By year-end, each sibling had completed two assignments, the council had adopted the role profiles and the family left with tools that they could continue using by themselves.

Process matters as much as product. Advisers should work against clear milestones (eg, role profiles and competencies agreed, meeting cadence set and first development plans in place) and leave behind tools that the family can keep using without them, including templates, rubrics and debrief guides. The office can coordinate logistics, but advisers should report to the appropriate governance forum, not 'go around' it. Boundaries protect relationships. Advisory work aimed at development is not therapy; sensitivities may surface, but the focus remains on roles, behaviours and decisions.

Process matters as much as product. Advisers should work against clear milestones (eg, role profiles and competencies agreed, meeting cadence set and first development plans in place) and leave behind tools that the family can keep using without them, including templates, rubrics and debrief guides.

Finally, plan for exit from the start. A short pilot with defined deliverables (eg, a one-page decision protocol and two tested role profiles) helps families to learn quickly whether the fit is right. The test of value is simple: did decisions improve, did participation broaden and did the family gain tools that they can use without the adviser? If yes, renew or extend; if not, close cleanly and move on.

11. Two composite cases

11.1 Case A: Founder with three very different adult children

A first-generation founder had built a substantial enterprise and expected his three adult children to 'step up' as future owners. Their starting points were uneven. The eldest had received business training and had worked closely with their father; the second, a physician, felt distant from the commercial world but cared deeply about health innovation; the third had never found a stable path, lived with ADHD and had a deep-rooted sense of inferiority compared to their accomplished siblings. Initial financial literacy classes delivered by internal staff proved unsuccessful, as the siblings felt that these were too basic and disconnected from their reality. We began with work focused on identity and clarified pathways: not everyone needed to be an operating executive. A coached conversation linked the physician's interest to a small venture-style health project; while the third sibling scoped a philanthropic initiative in a field they already cared about, within clear guardrails. The work became meaningful and concrete, and learning happened through practice. The siblings met monthly to share decisions and reflections using a simple debrief template (aim, decision, reasons, learning). The eldest was relieved of the tacit expectation to 'carry' the generation alone; while the founder saw visible progress without forcing roles. Over two years, capability evened out: the physician became an informed owner-advocate for a medical venture, while the third sibling developed confidence through grant cycles and now contributes calmly to owner discussions. This arc reflects a broader principle: place knowledge before power and pair capability building with purpose so that commitment becomes voluntary and durable.[36]

11.2 Case B: Dispersed cousins finding their footing as owners

In another family, G2 had long dominated decisions. G3 cousins lived in several different countries, knew little of the enterprise and were often described as 'not ready'. A health scare for a key G2 leader exposed a governance gap: there was no practical way to take decisions if two or three people were suddenly absent. The family began with a brief statement of purpose and a short charter that linked values to simple meeting norms. A calendar of quarterly owner forums mixed context briefings with case-style discussions; each session opened with a minute of reflection and turn-taking was followed so that quieter voices could be heard. G3's involvement stepped up over time: first observe; then submit a brief; then present a recommendation. In parallel, a modest owner apprenticeship programme offered coached goal-setting, curated reading and defined roles on a philanthropy or investment subgroup with a single sponsor and clear feedback. The office coordinated logistics and kept a light development log so that progress was visible without becoming bureaucratic. By the end of 12 months, the cousins were leading a small test portfolio on digitisation themes that they had identified and a junior grants round that brought the purpose to life. The temperature in meetings dropped as process fairness improved. G2's confidence in G3 increased because contribution was now observable against agreed expectations, rather than assumed from pedigree or dismissed for inexperience. In short, governance became a classroom and capability grew through doing.[37]

12. Conclusion

Families that are meticulous about tax, structures and investment policy should be equally systematic about developing the rising generation. This work is integrated and collaborative: family leaders, the family office and external advisers must each play a defined part. Roles should be clarified. Expectations should be visible. Learning should be lived, captured and shared.

The opportunity is clear: families that begin early, place knowledge before power and use governance as a classroom create engaged owners and steady successors. These outcomes are not accidental; they follow commitment to people, process and purpose over time.

Figure 1: 'Knowledge-before-power' runway

Exposure ➡ Contribution ➡ Authority (+ feedback loop)

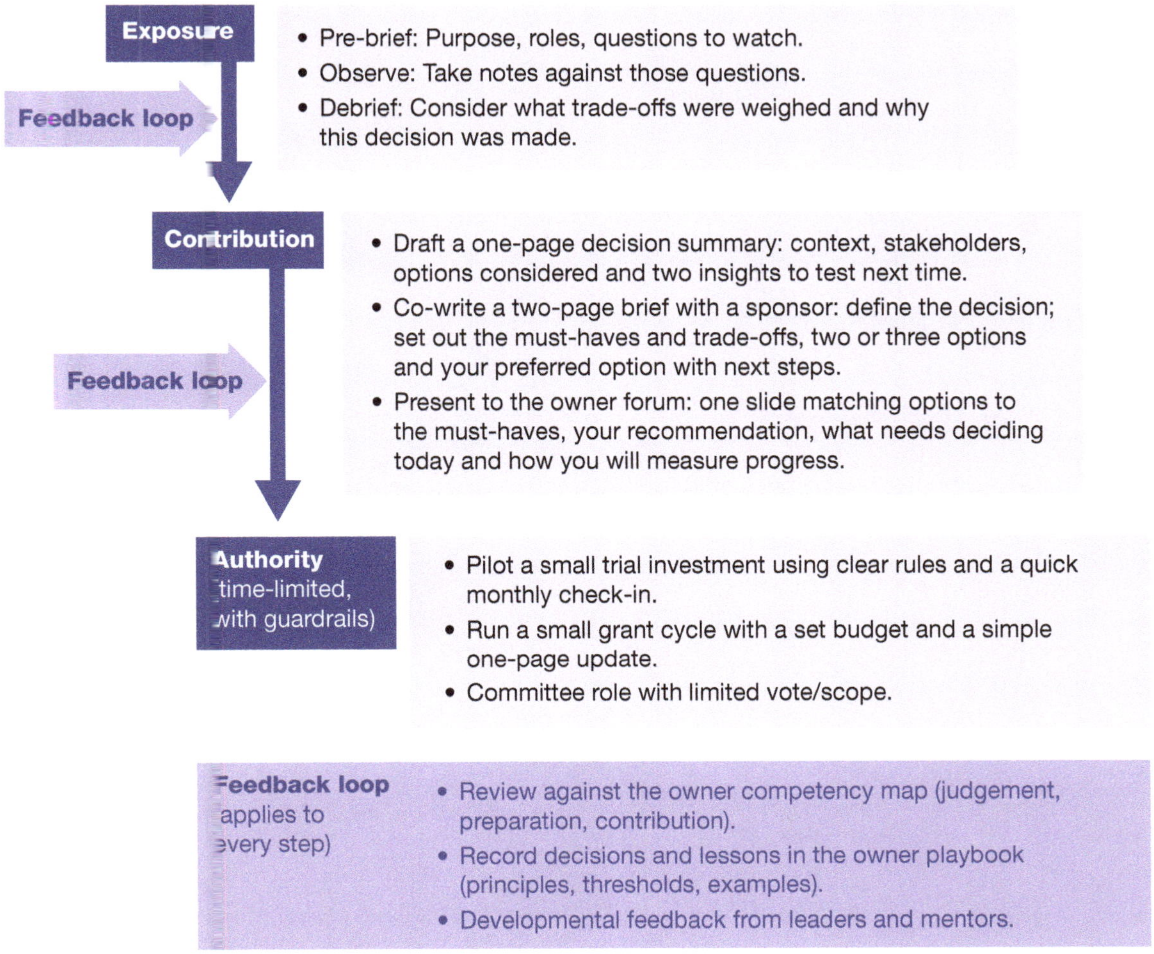

Source: Author's framework, informed by Jaffe (2007).

Notes

1 Northern Trust, "Engaging the Rising Gen: Practical Advice from Future Family Leaders and Family Office Execs", 2024, www.northerntrust.com/content/dam/northerntrust/events/documents/engaging-the-rising-gen-research.pdf.
2 Campden Wealth and AlTi Tiedemann Global, *The Family Office Operational Excellence Report* 2025, www.campdenwealth.com/report/family-office-operational-excellence-report-2025.
3 Northern Trust, "Engaging the Rising Gen: Practical Advice from Future Family Leaders and Family Office Execs", 2024, www.northerntrust.com/content/dam/northerntrust/events/documents/engaging-the-rising-gen-research.pdf.
4 DT Jaffe, "Knowledge before power – handing over the firm", *Families in Business*, September/October 2007, pp60–61, https://dennisjaffe.com/download/knowledge-before-power-handing-over-the-firm/.
5 Northern Trust, "Engaging the Rising Gen: Practical Advice from Future Family Leaders and Family Office Execs", 2024, www.northerntrust.com/content/dam/northerntrust/events/documents/engaging-the-rising-gen-research.pdf.
6 Rhian-Anwen Hamill, Maya Prabhu and Marie-Thérèse Yates, "Hiring leaders for the family office" in *Family Offices: The STEP Handbook for Advisers* (3rd edn, 2023), pp157–175.
7 Campden Wealth and AlTi Tiedemann Global, *The Family Office Operational Excellence Report 2025*, www.campdenwealth.com/report/family-office-operational-excellence-report-2025.
8 Rhian-Anwen Hamill, Maya Prabhu and Marie-Thérèse Yates, "Hiring leaders for the family office" in *Family Offices: The STEP Handbook for Advisers* (3rd edn, 2023), pp157–175.
9 Campden Wealth and AlTi Tiedemann Global, *The Family Office Operational Excellence Report 2025*, www.campdenwealth.com/report/family-office-operational-excellence-report-2025.
10 DT Jaffe, "Good Fortune: Building a Hundred-Year Family Enterprise", Wise Counsel Research, August 2013, pp9–18, https://fbrc.com.au/__static/d1ba95080f8dafbb8fac7ca1894ec8cb/130921-building-a-100-yr-fam-enterprise-2.pdf.

11 S Hamilton, "Great Family Legacies Are No Accident of History", *The European Financial Review*, 24 August 2011, www.europeanfinancialreview.com/great-family-legacies-are-no-accident-of-history/.
12 Campden Wealth and AlTi Tiedemann Global, *The Family Office Operational Excellence Report 2025*, www.campdenwealth.com/report/family-office-operational-excellence-report-2025.
13 DT Jaffe, "Good Fortune: Building a Hundred-Year Family Enterprise", Wise Counsel Research, August 2013, pp9–18, https://fbrc.com.au/__static/d1ba9508of8dafbb8fac7ca1894ec8cb/130921-building-a-100-yr-fam-enterprise-2.pdf.
14 Northern Trust, "Engaging the Rising Gen: Practical Advice from Future Family Leaders and Family Office Execs", 2024, www.northerntrust.com/content/dam/northerntrust/events/documents/engaging-the-rising-gen-research.pdf.
15 DT Jaffe, "Knowledge before power – handing over the firm", *Families in Business*, September/October 2007, pp60–61, https://dennisjaffe.com/download/knowledge-before-power-handing-over-the-firm/.
16 Northern Trust, "Engaging the Rising Gen: Practical Advice from Future Family Leaders and Family Office Execs", 2024, www.northerntrust.com/content/dam/northerntrust/events/documents/engaging-the-rising-gen-research.pdf.
17 R Carlock and JL Ward, *Strategic Planning for the Family Business* (Palgrave Macmillan, 2001), pp127–131.
18 DT Jaffe and JA Grubman, "Acquirers' and Inheritors' Dilemma: Discovering Life Purpose and Building Personal Identity in the Presence of Wealth", *The Journal of Wealth Management*, Fall 2007, 16–24, https://jamesgrubman.com/wp-content/uploads/2025/01/2007-Acquirers-and-Inheritors-Jaffe-Grubman-JWM-secure.pdf.
19 Campden Wealth and AlTi Tiedemann Global, *The Family Office Operational Excellence Report 2025*, www.campdenwealth.com/report/family-office-operational-excellence-report-2025.
20 PJ Weil, "Let's Do It the SMART Way: A Practical Guide for the Raising of Affluent Children", September 2017, www.pjweil.com/wp-content/uploads/2017/11/Family-Offices-Journal-fifth-edition-Philippe-J-Weil.pdf.
21 Campden Wealth and AlTi Tiedemann Global, *The Family Office Operational Excellence Report 2025*, www.campdenwealth.com/report/family-office-operational-excellence-report-2025.
22 *Ibid.*
23 DT Jaffe and James A Grubman, "Acquirers' and Inheritors' Dilemma: Discovering Life Purpose and Building Personal Identity in the Presence of Wealth", *The Journal of Wealth Management*, Fall 2007, 16–24, https://jamesgrubman.com/wp-content/uploads/2025/01/2007-Acquirers-and-Inheritors-Jaffe-Grubman-JWM-secure.pdf.
24 Campden Wealth and AlTi Tiedemann Global, *The Family Office Operational Excellence Report 2025*, www.campdenwealth.com/report/family-office-operational-excellence-report-2025.
25 *Ibid*. See also DT Jaffe, "Good Fortune: Building a Hundred-Year Family Enterprise", Wise Counsel Research, August 2013, pp9–18, https://fbrc.com.au/__static/d1ba9508of8dafbb8fac7ca1894ec8cb/130921-building-a-100-yr-fam-enterprise-2.pdf.
26 *Ibid.*
27 *Ibid.*
28 Campden Wealth and AlTi Tiedemann Global, *The Family Office Operational Excellence Report 2025*, www.campdenwealth.com/report/family-office-operational-excellence-report-2025.
29 Rhian-Anwen Hamill, Maya Prabhu and Marie-Thérèse Yates, "Hiring leaders for the family office" in *Family Offices: The STEP Handbook for Advisers* (3rd edn, 2023), pp157–175.
30 DT Jaffe, "Good Fortune: Building a Hundred-Year Family Enterprise", Wise Counsel Research, August 2013, pp9–18, https://fbrc.com.au/__static/d1ba9508of8dafbb8fac7ca1894ec8cb/130921-building-a-100-yr-fam-enterprise-2.pdf.
31 Andrew Likierman, *Judgement at Work: Making Better Choices* (Profile Books 2025), www.amazon.co.uk/Judgement-Work-Making-Better-Choices/dp/1805223526.
32 Rhian-Anwen Hamill, Maya Prabhu and Marie-Thérèse Yates, "Hiring leaders for the family office" in *Family Offices: The STEP Handbook for Advisers* (3rd edn, 2023), pp157–175.
33 *Ibid.*
34 Campden Wealth and AlTi Tiedemann Global, *The Family Office Operational Excellence Report 2025*, www.campdenwealth.com/report/family-office-operational-excellence-report-2025.
35 Rhian-Anwen Hamill, Maya Prabhu and Marie-Thérèse Yates, "Hiring leaders for the family office" in *Family Offices: The STEP Handbook for Advisers* (3rd edn, 2023), pp157–175.
36 DT Jaffe, "Knowledge before power – handing over the firm", *Families in Business*, September/October 2007, pp60–61, https://dennisjaffe.com/download/knowledge-before-power-handing-over-the-firm/.
37 DT Jaffe, "Good Fortune: Building a Hundred-Year Family Enterprise", Wise Counsel Research, August 2013, 9–18, https://fbrc.com.au/__static/d1ba9508of8dafbb8fac7ca1894ec8cb/130921-building-a-100-yr-fam-enterprise-2.pdf. See also R Carlock and JL Ward, *Strategic Planning for the Family Business*, (Palgrave Macmillan, 2001), pp127–131.

III. Beyond the inheritor: addressing the family system in next-generation education

Jessica McGawley
Dallington
Sonya Gladstone
Rhian-Anwen Hamill
RAH Partners

1. Introduction

Preparing the next generation in families of substantial means is a critical task for parents and advisers alike. Nowadays, there are many high-quality education programmes addressing topics such as financial literacy and board governance. However, young people will never be fully prepared for ownership, leadership and stewardship without engaging their parents and the full family system in issues that go beyond what can be taught in a classroom to improve understanding and technical skills. It is our contention that families should address the psychological and relational patterns embedded in the family structure with equal care and attention. Preparing the next generation must also involve preparing previous generations, yet this crucial step is often not taken by significant families.

When family patterns are left unaddressed, they inevitably manifest in the boardroom, the family office or the asset allocation meeting. While an individual-focused approach is necessary for creating responsible future leaders, it should be combined with work across the entire family. As family advisers – on both human capital broadly and next generations specifically – we have come together to share how we advise families to work with all generations and to provide an actionable approach to working with the family system in its entirety.

In section 2 below, we outline the need for parental engagement and explore the psychological hurdles that holding generations must overcome. We examine how to create the space necessary for the next generation to grow independently, addressing the cultural gap between generations and the systemic risks of parental judgement, favouritism and scapegoating. By helping parents to 'switch hats' from business leaders to self-aware emotional supporters, families can smooth transitions and dismantle roadblocks that hinder communication.

Then, in section 3, we explore the development required to move from individual inheritors to a cohesive cohort. We begin by discussing the essential work with the individual that must come first, establishing agency through protected training forums – practical experiences that build self-esteem and redefine resourcefulness as stewardship. We then examine working with siblings or cousins to create cohesion as a group, fostering peer-to-peer relationships through shared experiences and creating the relational muscle needed for future collaborative leadership.

Finally, in section 4, we provide a framework for long-term family success. We examine how purposeful education builds a common

By helping parents to 'switch hats' from business leaders to self-aware emotional supporters, families can smooth transitions and dismantle roadblocks that hinder communication.

language. This approach acknowledges that differences are inevitable and focuses on 'holding' those individual perspectives while striving for a 'united front'. By utilising the adviser as a bridge, a facilitator, an honest broker and a 'translator' – and by turning family governance into an evolving process via a charter that can develop and change over time – families can move beyond parallel lives and into a shared strategic dialogue, giving the next generation the best chance to lead as a competent, unified team.

2. Working with parents

2.1 The importance of parental engagement: beyond the individual

Preparing the rising generation for the complexities of ownership and leadership is a systemic imperative. It is rarely possible to effectively prepare young adults for these responsibilities without active parental engagement and a rigorous examination of the psychological and relational patterns embedded within the family structure. In our advisory work, we aim to guide parents in providing the necessary emotional support and 'daylight' required for the next generation to cultivate independent agency.

This can be considered through the metaphor of a great tree: when a dominant founder's success, like the crown of a great oak, casts dense shade below, little or no light can reach the ground. While the founder's dominance is often the driver of the family's wealth, it can, if not addressed, inadvertently stifle the development of the very successors for whom so much is hoped and in whose success parents are so invested.

As advisers, we help parents to recognise that the specific traits responsible for their commercial success (eg, resourcefulness born of necessity, relentless problem-solving and drive) can become inhibitory when applied to the next generation. While the first generation often utilised work as a primary means of navigating difficult circumstances, their children are growing up in a very different environment that does not naturally demand that same level of grit.

We frequently observe that a family leader may instinctively try to solve every problem for their children or apply the same high-pressure tactics that fuelled their own success. This not only limits the 'light' available for these individuals to grow but can fundamentally undermine the successors' self-esteem and confidence. Teaching a parent to effectively 'switch hats', transitioning from exceptional businessperson to emotional supporter invested in a child's agency (at any age), growth and self-determination, is vital to work past the unintended consequences of a highly successful older generation.

2.2 The cultural gap

The transition from the first generation (G1) to the second (G2) is arguably the most significant cultural and psychological hurdle in a family's history. Historically, G1 comes from a background in which resourcefulness was a response to necessity. Need is a great driver! Their resilience was honed in circumstances that demanded hands-on problem solving and the direct management of practical challenges – the traits that underpinned their eventual commercial success. In contrast, G2 is frequently raised within an affluent environment where need is not present. Often educated at private institutions and supported by staff, G2 may be shielded from the everyday stressors that elicited the previous generation's resilience, reaching adulthood without having needed to solve significant problems independently.

In our work, we have observed that this dynamic frequently prompts parents to label the rising generation as 'entitled' or 'incapable'. However, we would contend that parents must acknowledge their own part in creating the environment that has led to this perceived lack of readiness. When parents intervene to solve every challenge, they inadvertently bolster their own feelings of competence while robbing the child of the opportunity to develop true agency and a sense of ownership.

We have found that long-term success is more likely when parents learn to 'sit alongside' a child facing a problem rather than stepping in to provide the solution. This requires G1 to consciously step back from their role as the 'boss' within the home. The assertive, and at times aggressive, posture required to build a global empire can be inadvertently damaging when applied to parenting and inhibits the development of future owners.

2.3 Parental judgement and the problem of scapegoating

Another hurdle in family systems is the problem of scapegoating. When a family identifies a 'family contrarian', it is rarely a reflection of that individual alone; rather, it is a symptom of a system that needs one. Scapegoating allows the broader family to avoid a rigorous moral inventory of their own collective behaviours. Frequently, the designated scapegoat acts as a container for the family's unresolved frustrations or mirrors traits, such as ruthlessness, that the parents have yet to acknowledge in themselves.

We often see instances where an individual is being scapegoated. For example, a child may have a different communication style and be the 'family contrarian' because of it. Yet this individual is the only member of the system being consistently honest and refusing to play by the unspoken family 'rules'. By focusing on the 'delivery' as the problem, the family system avoids the uncomfortable truths being presented.

When parents intervene to solve every challenge, they inadvertently bolster their own feelings of competence while robbing the child of the opportunity to develop true agency and a sense of ownership.

It is vital to recognise the vacuum effect: if a 'family contrarian' is removed or 'fixed' without addressing the underlying system, the family will often subconsciously appoint a successor, as the system requires a designated person to hold its frustrations.

To overcome these roadblocks, advisers must carefully call them out – regardless of initial discomfort – to prevent the family from 'othering' their own members and to encourage collective accountability. This supports our contention that engagement of the full family system is vital.

Additionally, families should move towards more transparent processes and objective, merit-based systems for determining roles. This provides an external professionalised process to support and, if necessary, challenge parental judgement. Establishing a principles and protocols document that serves as the family charter or constitution is important and this should be treated as a living entity that each generation is empowered to adapt.

The adviser's key role in this process is that of 'translator': an individual who can navigate the cultural gap between generations by speaking both the language of business logic and the language of family psychology. These advisers serve as a bridge between the legal counsel often used to draft constitutions and the emotional needs of the family system.

By involving the rising generation in the evolution of these governance structures, we can ensure that they are not alienated by a framework established before they reached adulthood. Simultaneously, this helps the holding generation to develop the requisite confidence to adopt the necessary change.

Ultimately, the success of frameworks such as objective role determination and the inclusive creation of a family constitution will depend on whether the next generation is properly equipped to operate within them. Parental adjustment is the first half of the equation; the second requires the rising generation to operate in these systems, moving beyond individual competition and embracing the role of collective stewards. By focusing first on the individual and then on the relational health of the cohort, we can transform potential barriers into a pathway for future collaborative leadership.

3. Working with the next generation

3.1 Developing agency

While section 2 of this chapter addressed the need for the holding generation to create 'daylight', the rising generation must also learn how to grow within it. Because G2 is often raised in a shielded environment, many reach adulthood with a deficit in perceived competence; they often have quiet doubt in their own capabilities because they have never been required to test their resourcefulness against real-world problems.

To bridge this gap, work with the next generation should focus on reclaiming agency through protected training grounds and should be addressed on an individual basis before moving to work with a group of siblings or cousins. This involves low-stakes environments designed for trial and error, such as philanthropy committees or mock boards. The adviser works with each member individually, discussing problems that they have faced or questions that may have arisen for them, allowing them to feel they are in a safe and honest space where such ventilation is encouraged. In these settings, the objective is not a financial return, but a developmental return. This is where successors learn to navigate the weight of decision making and gain the critical realisation that they can survive, and learn from, professional failure.

This process requires a fundamental redefinition of 'resourcefulness'. In many families, the gold standard is the founder's 'scrappy' entrepreneurialism. However, the next generation is rarely in a position to build from nothing; instead, their primary challenge is one of stewardship. Once the adviser has helped the individual to build their own agency, they can begin to work on creating and developing the relational muscle required to move from being an individual creator to becoming a collective steward, working to ensure the long-term sustainability of the family.

3.2 Building peer-to-peer relationships through shared experience

Once individuals begin to develop personal agency, the focus must shift to the cohort. Successful transitions in a family enterprise require a move beyond individual competition towards a cohesive group identity. We often see how unaddressed sibling rivalry can inhibit a smooth transition; to dismantle this, the family must prioritise shared experiences that allow members to get to know one another outside of their roles as 'inheritors'.

These experiences are most effective when led by a neutral adviser who acts as a facilitator and an honest broker. The adviser creates a 'buffer zone': a protected emotional environment in which family members can engage in mutual vulnerability without fear of judgement.

One powerful way to foster this engagement is to provide the rising generation with dedicated forums in which every individual has a voice.

Successful transitions in a family enterprise require a move beyond individual competition towards a cohesive group identity.

Take, for example, a cohort of six cousins from three distinct family branches: despite being future co-stewards, their interactions may have been limited to holidays or complicated by differing geographies and personalities. To bridge this gap, a family might establish a biannual next-generation forum: a long weekend in an engaging location designed to build collaboration. Within this protected emotional environment, an adviser can facilitate group discussions where contribution is not just encouraged but required. By balancing the input of introverted members with the practice of active listening across the group, the cohort can develop the collaborative thinking and collective decision-making skills that are essential for their future roles.

This development of collaboration is not only beneficial to their leadership but also of value in today's digital era. The rising generation is maturing under the constant shadow of public scrutiny; the anxiety of a potential public error can be paralysing. A facilitated and honest safe space helps siblings to appreciate one another and recognise their shared goals and challenges, moving the metric of success from individual grit to collective resilience. Many of the decisions that the next generation must make will be ones that must be made together and that will 'stick'. By fostering peer-to-peer relationships early and often, advisers and families can build the 'relational muscle' required for future collaborative leadership and unified ownership.

By fostering peer-to-peer relationships early and often, advisers and families can build the 'relational muscle' required for future collaborative leadership and unified ownership.

4. Creating a path forward: dialogue and education

4.1 Purposeful education – accepting differences and developing a common language

As we have emphasised, preparing the next generation is not a solo endeavour; it requires the entire family system to learn a new way of communicating. Meaningful education must extend beyond basic financial literacy. While understanding a balance sheet is a baseline requirement, the more critical education involves helping the family to develop a common language to discuss their human capital.

In this process, we must understand and accept that difference is inevitable. Education is not a tool to force consensus, but a means of establishing a way to hold difference while still aiming for a united front. When parents and siblings share a factual basis for understanding family psychology, they can move beyond reacting to old scripts and start addressing challenges – such as entitlement or rivalry – as systemic hurdles rather than individual character flaws.

This educational process also serves to break down the isolation that often accompanies significant wealth. We encourage families to seek out peer learning experiences, aligning with other families that have experienced similar complexities. Whether it is managing technology use or setting expectations for professional merit, parents often find it more effective to navigate these stressors when they have a peer network to work through them together.

For the rising generation, this shared journey is transformative because it shifts the focus from perceived deficits to their potential as collective stewards. By engaging in learning alongside their parents and peers, they realise that the pressures they feel – the weight of expectation and the fear of failure – are not unique to them, but rather a natural outcome of their environment. This realisation reduces the shame that some inheritors feel about significant wealth and replaces it with a sense of belonging to a community. Ultimately, purposeful education provides successors with the vocabulary to advocate for their own development and the confidence to engage with the holding generation as informed, capable partners.

4.2 Strategic dialogue and the adviser as translator

The ultimate objective of this systemic work is to move the family from parallel lives to a shared strategic dialogue. As we have explored, the holding generation often operates within a framework of individual grit, while the rising generation matures in an environment of high-stakes public scrutiny and shielded development. To bridge this gap, families require more than legal structures and financial education; they need a translator and a conduit.

By utilising the adviser as an honest broker and facilitator, families can periodically revisit this framework to ensure that it reflects the current reality of the cohort's evolving skills and interests.

Family members are often too close to their own history to objectively identify risks such as the 'great tree' or scapegoating. The adviser's role is to facilitate a fearless moral inventory of the entire system, encouraging each member to examine their contribution to the collective dynamic rather than pointing fingers at the 'family contrarian'.

This ongoing dialogue finds its formal structure in what we have termed the 'living charter'. While the initial stages of work involved removing subjective parental judgement, the true value of the charter is realised when it becomes the primary vehicle for the family's shared future. It must be seen as a dynamic roadmap that requires the next generation's active input and participation to remain relevant.

By utilising the adviser as an honest broker and facilitator, families can periodically revisit this framework to ensure that it reflects the current reality of the cohort's evolving skills and interests. This turns governance into a proactive exercise in collective stewardship rather than a reactive response to parental mandates. When the rising generation sees their own agency reflected in the family's governance, the charter ceases to be a barrier to entry, instead becoming a source of pride and professional self-worth. It transforms the enterprise from a legacy that they received into something that they are actively choosing to lead as a unified team.

5. Conclusion: investing in the whole family

Ultimately, preparing the next generation is not a matter of an individual's skill set or the technical knowledge of finances; it is about building the ultimate shared asset – a united, resilient and well-equipped family system.

Throughout our work, we have observed that the most successful transitions occur when families have the courage to identify where they may have fallen short in the parenting domain and seek the necessary guidance to navigate their unique complexities. This requires a shift in perspective: moving away from the idea that the next generation is a 'problem' to be solved and instead recognising the family as a collective entity that must evolve together.

There is no shame in acknowledging that the exceptional skills required to build a global empire are fundamentally different from the skills required to raise its successors. While G1 is defined by the grit and relentless drive needed to create wealth, G2 and G3 must cultivate the relational intelligence and consensus-building skills needed to manage it as a cohesive cohort. True success in wealth transition is realised when the 'great tree' provides the room necessary for 'daylight' and growth, and when the rising generation is given the protected space to establish their own voice of stewardship. It is in this 'daylight' that they can move from being passive inheritors to active, engaged owners.

When parents and successors are in the same room, speaking a common language and addressing systemic patterns together, the enterprise moves beyond the risks of individual failure and the fragility of sibling rivalry. By strengthening the relationships between generations and shifting the focus from fixing the individual to reinforcing the system, the family legacy is not just preserved; it is actively revitalised. This systemic approach ensures that the family remains as robust as the business it built, capable of weathering the challenges of the generations to come.

Family businesses and family offices share several characteristics with high-performance sports teams. Both are driven by unity of purpose, trust and, eventually, considerations of their legacy. Both depend on individuals who must balance rivalry and collaboration, competing internally while pulling towards a common goal.

IV. What high-performance sport can teach families: leadership, teamwork and individual talent

Colby Richardson
Blue Forge Capital
Sonya Gladstone
Rhian-Anwen Hamill
RAH Partners

1. Introduction

Family businesses and family offices share several characteristics with high-performance sports teams. Both are driven by unity of purpose, trust and, eventually, considerations of their legacy. Both depend on individuals who must balance rivalry and collaboration, competing internally while pulling towards a common goal. These shared traits can generate powerful outcomes[1] but also create unique challenges that can be difficult to navigate successfully.

We have observed significant parallels between the world of sport and the dynamics within family enterprises. To toot our own horns for a moment: before becoming involved in the world of family enterprise, we were once athletes – one might even say of the *elite* variety. Colby, a member of a multi-generation Canadian family business, rowed for the men's crew team at Brown University, one of the most competitive US collegiate rowing programmes. Sonya was a coxswain for Yale University's men's crew team – then the leading collegiate programme in the United States – and later for Leander Club's men's crew, the most successful single-sport club in the world, before joining RAH Partners to advise families alongside Rhian-Anwen Hamill, who has also kindly contributed to writing this chapter.

In this chapter, we draw on lessons learned from our sporting careers on how high-performance sports teams and coaches create success and consider how these apply to family enterprises dealing with many of the same complexities.

The chapter covers three key lessons:

- collective vision and leadership;
- trust created through:
    - meritocracy and transparency; and
    - care and value of the individual; and
- feedback and learning from failure.

The exploration is informed by multiple perspectives – specifically:

- our experiences and reflections upon reliving our sporting glory years;
- discussions with family business owners;
- insights from renowned coaches and athletes; and
- the growing body of research on family enterprises,[2] leadership, management and sports psychology.

Ultimately, our aim is to deepen understanding of human dynamics by examining lessons learned across all domains. Whether in sport,

Whether in sport, business or family enterprise, success depends on understanding and engaging with the people who make up the team.

business or family enterprise, success depends on understanding and engaging with the people who make up the team. As a *Forbes* article examining insights from four leading British football and rugby coaches observes: "The elite sports leader must create a vision, set a strategy, and recruit the right people for the team's success. In fact, the single-most defining feature connecting elite sports and business leadership is about understanding people."[3]

With this understanding in mind, the following sections examine key lessons from sports leadership that can help family enterprise members and advisers to build enduring, high-performance teams.

2. Lesson I: Collective vision

> *Teamwork is the ability to work together toward a common vision … It is the fuel that allows common people to attain uncommon results.*
> *Scottish-American industrialist Andrew Carnegie, who amassed one of the largest fortunes in US history with the expansion of the US steel industry. A dedicated philanthropist, he funded the creation of Lake Carnegie, designed specifically for the Princeton University rowing team, among many other projects.*

In sport, collective vision is at the heart of what motivates truly high-performance teams. When an individual's ambition is used to work towards collective success, beyond personal achievements, amazing things can happen. The power of a collective goal gives team members a sense of belonging, pride and the knowledge that their efforts are contributing to something enduring and meaningful.

Alistair Hargreaves and Chris Wyles, former players for London's premier rugby union team, have emphasised the importance of larger vision to both business and teams: "It's not just about the bricks – the people – but about the mortar; the things that bond them together."[4]

For professional athletes, the collective goal is often rooted in a national or regional pride. Gareth Southgate, former manager of England's football team, described his focus on connecting his team to their larger purpose: "This means being clear about what the white English shirt stands for, its heritage and its connection with both fans and the wider nation."[5]

One family member – the owner and chairperson of a professional football team – described how their club had become the custodian of the area's legacy: "All the industry left the region, but the football club stayed, so it was down to us to create the positive memories for the community, to create a legacy, a memory the community could be proud of."

Collective vision can bring together not just a team, but an entire nation, as illustrated in South Africa. During the 1995 Rugby World Cup, the Springboks united a newly democratic South Africa (the 'Rainbow Nation', as coined by Archbishop Desmond Tutu). Perhaps a lofty example for corporate teambuilding, but it illustrates how a clear and unifying vision can break down barriers and transform a group of individuals into a cohesive unit.

Personal reflections

Sonya Gladstone's experience as a collegiate rower at Yale demonstrates how a coach's articulation of purpose forged deep commitment, endurance and collective pride.

Every season, on the first day of training, Sonya's coach made a statement that carried her team through every moment in which extraordinary motivation was required:

> *Our goal is to win every race and we train to win. But we do not endeavour to win for personal glory. We train for everyone sitting in this room, and for the individuals who laid down the path of durability, strength and effort that you now reap the benefits of. You are now the stewards of this legacy and the backbones of each other. The less the process is about yourself, the better off you will be.*

While the phrase 'personal glory' may not be as applicable to the boardroom as it was to a team of 18–22 university men, the clarity in outlining collective purpose that Sonya's coach displayed is worthwhile noting.

This idea of a collective vision was particularly salient for Sonya, because the coach who delivered this speech was also her father Steve Gladstone. Rowing, for the Gladstones, is their family business. As the only child in their family who showed interest in the sport, Sonya grew up understanding that what it meant to carry the Gladstone name went far beyond any one individual her father coached. His 14 national titles made Steve the most successful American collegiate rowing coach in history (technically, he is tied as the most successful rowing coach in American history with Charles Courtney of Cornell, 1883–1920; but that was a long time ago and collegiate athletics was not as competitive back then, according to Steve).

The true power of Steve's uniting force was captured by one athlete from his time at the University of California, Berkeley, who noted "When you meet another person coached by Steve, you have the feeling you share DNA. His lessons transformed my life – transformed generations of college rowers across America."

The power of a collective vision, as this rower illustrated, can make its followers feel like family. Steve reinforced the importance of the collective legacy of each team he coached. While he repeated the same sentiment each week – particularly when the training was at its most gruelling – Sonya never forgot the first time he spoke it to the team she was a part of. The individual's role in this larger legacy was clearly outlined and the motivation to train came from something far greater than her individual resolve: the pursuit of the team's success.

We confess that, nuance aside, rowing is like many sports in that it has a rather straightforward goal: make it to the finish line, every time, before every other crew does. The difficulty is in justifying why the tremendous effort to do so is worthwhile. The importance of collective vision and purpose is highlighted by leadership psychologist and author Simon Sinek in his bestselling book *Start with Why: How Great Leaders Inspire Everyone to Take Action.*[6]

Sinek contends that the most inspiring and impactful way to begin when creating a successful business is to "start with why". In his books, he describes the model of the 'golden circle', which places a mission at the core of success. He suggests that the most successful teams value individuals with high levels of trustworthiness over those who may have higher performance, because the former individuals can be counted on to hold the group's goals above their own.[7] Sinek's explicit 'callout' of trust as the key to making a collective vision actionable ties into the next lesson from sport.

Determining the collective goal for a family enterprise, while arguably more difficult, is no less vital. Clarifying family values is the first step towards determining a collective goal for a family. This process may involve writing or updating a family charter, constitution or mission/purpose statement. Bringing in an adviser who can help to guide the conversations on family history and values will aid in the process of determining what success means beyond financial returns.

From a written statement, families can discuss what their values look like in practice. For example, if one of the family values is responsibility, family members can have a guided conversation with an adviser about what the behaviours of a responsible owner look like in practice. Perhaps one family member believes that responsible ownership involves growing their wealth, while another believes that responsibility should encompass philanthropy in their community. No matter the outcome, these conversations illuminate what matters most to the individuals, which collectively determines the family's guiding vision. Just as a rowing crew must align every stroke towards the finish line, so too must families in business unite around common objectives that motivate beyond individual interests.

3. Lesson II: Trust

> Spectemur Agendo. *Let us be judged by our deeds.*
> *Inscription on the Varsity Challenge Trophy, one of the highest honours in collegiate men's heavyweight rowing.*

> *To be able to truly lead someone, you have to know them. Not the work colleague, not the player, but the real person behind that front.*
> *Will Carling, former English rugby union player, England's youngest captain and the longest-serving and most successful captain in the sport's history; now a business consultant and leadership mentor.*

Building on the importance of collective vision, the next lesson is trust – the foundation on which lasting teams are built.

Scholars of management theory have found that a lack of trust can be the biggest impediment to team success. In his book *The Five Dysfunctions of a Team*,[8] Patrick Lencioni argues that when trust is not present in a team, members will hide their mistakes and hesitate to ask for help. An inability to be vulnerable with colleagues frustrates collaboration and can lead to fear and insecurity.[9] In this environment, individual improvement is unlikely and motivation to work towards a collective vision is absent.

The importance of trust is also echoed in sports literature. In his highly popular *Harvard Business Review* article on lessons for business leaders, legendary American football quarterback Tom Brady writes: "[L]eadership requires trust, and trust usually comes from deeply caring about one another and the belief that winning is about the team."[10]

So, trust matters. Hardly a revolutionary concept in leadership, though building it authentically can prove challenging. The methods that we have seen employed in sport are, first, to create a culture of meritocracy and transparency; and second, to ensure that the individual is cared for and valued.

3.1 Meritocracy and transparency

In true high-performance teams, members understand how and why decisions are made. The individuals collaborate through a system in which an outcome is determined through a process that everyone understands and supports, even if they take issue with the decision.

For this to work, communication from leadership is paramount; and while it is not necessary for the coach or manager to justify every nuance of their thinking, those whom they oversee need to trust that their efforts are being valued and the decisions being made are in the interests of the group's collective vision.

One illustration of meritocracy in action comes from Colby's experience on Brown University men's crew team, showing how fairness, competition and accountability can build both individual excellence and collective trust.

Personal reflections

Colby Richardson recalls how every rowing practice offered an opportunity. The rowing programme at Brown University under coach Paul Cooke (formerly a rower and student under Steve Gladstone) was and continues to be renowned for its work ethic. In an era when the rival University of Washington dominated the stands at the Intercollegiate Rowing Association finals, the Brown University men's crew team adopted a 'pressure cooker' training regimen to stay competitive, emphasising volume and constant competition to hone the skills of its athletes. As gruelling as it was, interchanging the lineups (the team 'rosters') meant more chances of earning a spot in the top boats. This not only improved the odds of assembling a winning lineup but also boosted team morale in the face of difficult decisions.

One tried-and-true method of testing rowers against each other is the infamous seat race, in which two or more boats race side by side before switching athletes from one boat to another and racing again. As physically demanding as it is nerve-wracking, this imperfect test is conducted until a clear winner has been identified. Brown University crew's volume-intensive training meant long practices and many seat races. Colby and his crewmates were given more opportunity to compete for the top seats and no one rower's seat was guaranteed. Everything had to be earned.

Because of this demanding training regimen, whatever hierarchies existed broke down in the face of the effort required by each member of the team. At the end of each practice, everyone – whether they were in the first varsity or the fourth – was thoroughly exhausted. This collective effort towards a common goal lowered any social barriers and deepened the sense of camaraderie between the teammates. Nearly 20 years since joining the team at age 17, Colby still counts his teammates as some of his closest friends.

While many rowers from that era agree that the training regimen at

Brown University crew was spartan, their experience highlights a powerful theme in this chapter: an environment with a unifying purpose that rewards individual efforts can motivate its members to remarkable efforts; and in the course of this effort, camaraderie is developed in the pursuit of excellence. Colby's story highlights how transparent systems of evaluation – however demanding – strengthen not just performance but also the bonds within a team.

In a family enterprise, the practical application of this lesson is that performance-based advancement must coexist with the responsibilities and symbolism of family roles. To this end, leaders should consider implementing transparent evaluation systems that respect both performance and legacy. The simplicity of the rowing formula, where effort equates more immediately to success, is not easily replicable in business, though the value of creating a system in which members feel that their efforts are rewarded and worthwhile can be as significant.

When a team fosters the culture that Colby describes, enduring trust grows because the individuals witness the efforts of their teammates and rewards feel earned. When this level of unceasing competitiveness is combined with deep care for each other as individuals, authentic and lasting trust can be formed.

3.2 Care and value of the individual

Too often, in the relentless pursuit of results, teams – whether in sport or in family enterprise – fall into the trap of valuing individuals solely for their output. But the best coaches know their athletes not just as rowers, runners or players, but as whole individuals with unique motivations, strengths and vulnerabilities. True trust emerges when coaches and leaders care deeply about these people beyond just their performance.

Sports psychology research supports the importance of care as a defining feature of success. In examining the coach-athlete relationship, Misasi *et al* found that "the best way for a coach to lead an athlete to perform at a high level is to get to know them deeply and to work hard to understand their goals, motivations and needs".[11]

Leaders who see their team members as people first[12] and performers second build genuine connections that lead to trust between leader and athlete. This philosophy is echoed in the words of one family business principal and chairperson of a UK football club, who responded, when asked about core values that created their success: "It is all about the people. Often, fans can treat players like football automatons, but they are people who just happen to be football players."

Emotional intelligence in leadership is the key learning for families. In a family enterprise, it is easy to value one member's superior abilities in management above the potential and unique attributes of others. In a team, every member's contribution must be valued – especially by their leaders. The most caring leaders curate an ecosystem in which different abilities are accommodated and valued differently. Just like a rowing boat, everyone is pulling in the same direction, even if some are stronger than others.

This care can exist even in competitive environments. A delicate balance can be achieved in sport when the athlete understands that their coach cares for them as an individual first and their performance second. When the leader values effort and commitment more than winning and losing, the balance is struck.

When teams make emotional intelligence a core competency in leadership development – for example, by holding regular one-on-ones and creating safe channels for conversations beyond just performance evaluations – they are taking steps to develop this caring and trusting culture.[13] Like a great coach, family leaders should tune in to the motivations, struggles and aspirations of their people. This can bridge generational gaps, resolve tensions before they escalate and strengthen engagement from non-family leaders. When people feel seen and valued as individuals, they are more willing to invest themselves in the team.

Like a great coach, family leaders should tune in to the motivations, struggles and aspirations of their people. This can bridge generational gaps, resolve tensions before they escalate and strengthen engagement from non-family leaders.

3.3 In conclusion

In family enterprises, where relationships are layered with history and emotion, building trust can be more challenging than in sport. Family business research shows that trust – a competitive advantage in the early stages – often deteriorates as the firm grows, making consistent trust-building practices even more critical. Trust between family members, executives and advisers comes from reliability, transparency and fairness in decision making.

One second-generation UK family business leader reflected on his family's efforts to draft a constitution. He noted that the first attempts created 'business constitutions' that the next generation did not feel connected to. It was only when the family sat down, expressed their value and care for their next-generation members and listened to their voices as individuals beyond the business that they were able to craft a constitution that had true staying power.

This was not as easy as it sounds. Listening to the next generation meant inviting opinions that contrasted sharply with his own. He noted: "We respected their individual values, even when they took different forms from the values we had been raised with." This family's experience of how much more successful their governance process became once they took the time and care to listen to individual family members and understand their motivations is a powerful example of what care for individuals looks like in practice.

Family members should establish predictable, respectful forums for communication (eg, annual retreats and cross-generational planning days). When a family member may be too closely linked to act as described above, an adviser can help to create a trusting environment by facilitating conversations in which each member's voice can be heard in a safe and caring space mediated by the outside adviser.

Building and sustaining trust is a continual and intentional effort, bolstered by empathy, transparency and the prioritisation of relationships over hierarchy. Trust grows not from slogans or statements, but from consistent daily actions. Leaders must demonstrate genuine concern for each member's wellbeing and encourage their development. Through small actions in which leaders show care for team members, trust can be created and individuals will feel empowered to follow the collective vision. Once it is in place, trust creates an environment in which individuals can weather adversity.

Building and sustaining trust is a continual and intentional effort, bolstered by empathy, transparency and the prioritisation of relationships over hierarchy.

4. Lesson III: Learning from failure and the importance of feedback

> *When you're playing a point, it is the most important thing in the world. But when it's behind you, it's behind you ... The best in the world are not the best because they win every point ... It's because they know they'll lose ... again and again ... and have learned how to deal with it.*
>
> *Roger Federer, Swiss tennis player and winner of eight Wimbledon titles, in his 2024 commencement address at Dartmouth College.*

Building a foundation of trust, as outlined in the previous section, is not just about creating a caring environment because it is more comfortable; it is a vital prerequisite for continuous growth, especially when that growth requires vulnerability. Knowing that asking for help or admitting failure will not lead to any less care or perceived confidence allows team members to use failure as a tool for learning and progress.

As Roger Federer explains in the quote above, the best athletes learn how to take failure and just "deal with it".[14] Muhammad Ali captured the same idea when he said: "You don't lose if you get knocked down. You lose if you stay down."[15] This mindset – the deliberate 'dealing with it' that champions such as Federer advise – is what helps to transform setbacks into opportunities for organisational growth and continuous team evolution.

These athletes develop the mental resilience to learn from their failures because their team cultures not only normalise failure but also reward it with improvement. They operate on the assumption that they can always get better; and they trust their coaches to reward failure with feedback that will, in turn, make their performance stronger than it was before. Decorated British oarsman Alex Gregory discussed the importance of this open dialogue to his Olympic success. In an interview with the *Harvard Business Review* on performing under pressure, he described how his Olympic crew came together to learn "from all of us [in] the boat giving each other feedback".[16]

This idea of reframing setbacks has also been explained in psychology literature. Amy Edmondson, popular author and professor of leadership and management at Harvard Business School, discusses the importance of failure in her book *Right Kind of Wrong: The Science of Failing Well*.[17] When discussing a recent post-loss interview with tennis player Amanda Anisimova, Edmondson described Amanda's response as a "masterclass in failure ... she reframed the loss as an opportunity for growth". Edmondson goes on to suggest that athletes in general tend to understand the dynamic between failing and learning better than most. Edmondson again looks to a top tennis player in a post-match interview to explain this: when asked how he improved, Jannik Sinner said, "You just have to understand what you did wrong and you have to work on that."

In a family enterprise, this lesson of 'dealing with' failure facilitates growth when an individual trusts their leader to provide feedback, not punishment. For families to apply this lesson, the previous lessons of collective goals and trust must already have been implemented. Once there is a goal for the individual to work towards, failure turns from a personal wrongdoing into an opportunity for the individual to perform better in service of the group. When trust is established, failure and feedback become part of their daily routine of putting themselves out there, trusting that they are allowed to try even if they come up short of what they set out to do.

Again, this is not an easy lesson to implement; in practice, it takes a great deal of courage from the individual and understanding from the leader. Families can put this learning into practice by creating an environment in which trying and failing are acceptable with appropriate guardrails. For example, giving a next-generation family member early responsibilities with a business, a philanthropic endeavour or a sum of wealth that is significant but not fatal if lost, allows them to fail, learn and improve from the experience. When the family leader or adviser encourages this process of trial and error and is willing to provide feedback and work through the takeaways, they teach team members that the value is in the effort over the result. The next-generation members are then less afraid to propose an idea or to innovate because failure and feedback have been framed as tools for personal development.

Coach Steve Gladstone spoke to this balance, saying:

> *As a coach and a leader, you must understand the immense courage it takes for your athletes to endeavour to win ... When they come up short, be with them, comfort them, praise their courage, and once you have done that, offer feedback to help them improve the next time.*[18]

Former US President Theodore Roosevelt, in his "Citizens in a Republic" speech given in 1910, voiced a similar sentiment:

> *It is not the critic who counts ... The credit belongs to the man who is actually in the arena ... who errs, who comes short again and again, because there is no effort without error and shortcoming ... [The credit belongs to the man] who at the best knows in the end the triumph of high achievement, and who at the worst, if he fails, at least fails while daring greatly.*[19]

When family leaders and advisers can adopt this understanding, their team members can operate in an environment that rewards effort and courage and facilitates growth, making everyone in the system better as a result. The goal is not to avoid failure, but to design a family system that converts setbacks into intelligence. By replacing the fear of losing with the expectation of learning, family enterprises can ensure that every stumble becomes a powerful step towards long-term success.

5. Limitations: how elite sport and family business differ

Drawing parallels between business and sports has long been a popular framework for business scholars. Consider the metaphors employed in Jim Collins' *Good to Great*[20] or Ben Horowitz's *The Hard Thing about Hard Things*.[21] Notable articles in the *Harvard Business Review* have titles such as "Why Business is Like Baseball" or "What CEOs can Learn from Coaches". Michael Porter described his ubiquitous Five Forces in terminology such as "competitive advantage" and "playing field".[22] However, this comparison has also been criticised for its shortcomings.

In his 2016 *Harvard Business Review* article "Stop Comparing Management to Sports", Freek Vermeulen – professor of strategy and entrepreneurship at London Business School – argues that likening business to sports oversimplifies the strategic complexity of management and understates the importance of community and time in building great enterprises.[23] However, even Vermeulen admits that the sports analogy can help us to understand how successful teams set goals, overcome adversity and deal with disappointment.

Keen observers will have seen a problematic paradox of the sport-business metaphor when examining family enterprises. Family enterprises may operate like a sports team on the employee level, but their family executives and owners are typically irreplaceable as members of senior management. There are other ways in which the sport analogy falls short: business can be a lifelong pursuit, while competitive sport is often a fleeting, passion-filled endeavour favouring the young; and success in sport is often clearly defined, even binary, while success in business is rarely zero sum.

This notwithstanding, the three lessons from sport discussed in this chapter remain highly relevant.[24] For example, many elite sports teams have iconic leaders – figures such as Sir Alex Ferguson, Phil Jackson, Vince Lombardi and John Wooden – who become synonymous with the institution and have statues and stadiums in their name. This mirrors the challenge of managing powerful founder figures or principals within a family enterprise. Further, while the timeline of elite sport is often short-lived, the three lessons of collective vision, deep trust (through meritocracy and care) and learning from failure and feedback are ultimately applicable drivers for high performance and long-term sustainability in families and sports teams alike.

6. Conclusion

Family enterprises, much like high-performance sports teams, thrive when leaders cultivate an environment in which individual talent is encouraged and motivated by collective purpose, high trust and a focus on learning from failure. The lessons explored in this chapter provide some tools to improve team cohesion across generations. Further, these principles can serve as a framework for identifying and developing the next generation of leaders, helping to guide behaviours that translate values into action.

While the process of striving for high performance requires discipline and courage, it also benefits from an emotional and human dimension. Sustaining excellence over the long term depends on a sense of joy and connection that brings a team together. These lessons are often best supported when team members and leadership intentionally weave in moments of levity. Both Sonya and Colby recount many

Family enterprises, much like high-performance sports teams, thrive when leaders cultivate an environment in which individual talent is encouraged and motivated by collective purpose, high trust and a focus on learning from failure.

memories of light-hearted fun with their teammates. A core philosophy during Sonya's time on her university team was that while the work was serious, team members (and leadership) should never take themselves too seriously. Laughter and playfulness do a great deal to keep teams striving together.

These lessons are not just intellectual concepts; they require consistent, intentional application. Just as elite athletes understand that successful performance is the result of consistent practice, families must recognise that these principles are only as powerful as individuals are willing to implement them. Sustainable success, for athletes and family enterprise members alike, hinges on who their team members are and how they collaborate,[25] grow and support one another.

The opportunity for those who work in and around the family enterprise space is to cultivate an environment in which every person feels committed to the collective purpose. This commitment allows them to invest their energy and talent not only for their own achievement but also for the enduring legacy that they are preserving and shaping together. As families face the inevitable challenges of transition, changing external factors and setbacks, those who apply the lessons of high-performance sport will be best positioned to adapt, remain unified and create and adapt a successful new legacy for the future.

Notes

1 J Schwartz, I Roy, M Hauptmann, Y Van Durme and B Denny, "Organizational performance: It's a team sport: 2019 Global Human Capital Trends", Deloitte Insights, 2019, www.deloitte.com/us/en/insights/topics/talent/human-capital-trends/2019/team-based-organization.html.

2 V Ratten, "Family business and sport entrepreneurship," *Journal of Family Business Management*, September 2020; www.researchgate.net/publication/344016085_Family_business_and_sport_entrepreneurship B Salcinovic, M Drew, P Dijkstra *et al*, "Factors influencing team performance: What can support teams in high-performance sport learn from other industries? A systematic scoping review", *Sports Medicine – Open*, 8(25), 2022, https://doi.org/10.1186/s40798-021-00406-7.

3 Forrester, "Achieve high performance by learning from elite sports leaders", *Forbes*, 20 January 2022, www.forbes.com/sites/forrester/2022/01/20/achieve-high-performance-by-learning-from-elite-sports-leaders/.

4 "The sport of business: What small business owners can learn from athletes," *The Standard*, 6 August 2024, www.standard.co.uk/business/sport-business-small-business-owners-athletes-b1159252.html.

5 Forrester, "Achieve high performance by learning from elite sports leaders," *Forbes*, 20 January 2022, www.forbes.com/sites/forrester/2022/01/20/achieve-high-performance-by-learning-from-elite-sports-leaders/.

6 S Sinek, *Start with Why: How Great Leaders Inspire Everyone to Take Action* (Portfolio, 2009).

7 *Ibid.*

8 P Lencioni, *The Five Dysfunctions of a Team: A Leadership Fable* (Jossey-Bass, 2002).

9 *Ibid.*

10 T Brady and N Nohria, "Tom Brady on the art of leading teammates," *Harvard Business Review*, 102(5), 62–69, September–October 2024, https://hbr.org/2024/09/tom-brady-on-the-art-of-leading-teammates.

11 SP Misasi, G Morin and L Kwasnowski, "Leadership: Athletes and Coaches in Sport", *The Sport Journal*, 1 July 2016, https://thesportjournal.org/article/leadership-athletes-and-coaches-in-sport.

12 B Parcells, "The tough work of turning around a team", *Harvard Business Review*, November–December 2000, https://hbr.org/2000/11/the-tough-work-of-turning-around-a-team.

13 J Zenger and J Folkman, *The Inspiring Leader: Unlocking the Secret behind How Extraordinary Leaders Motivate* (Zenger Folkman, 2015), https://zengerfolkman.com/wp-content/uploads/2019/04/White-Paper_-Unlocking-The-Secret-Behind-How-Extraordinary-Leaders-Motivate.pdf.

14 M Fitzgerald, "Roger Federer's viral commencement speech: Lessons from the tennis legend's address at Dartmouth College", *The New York Times Athletic*, 10 June 2025, www.nytimes.com/athletic/6414410/2025/06/10/roger-federer-viral-commencement-speech_.

15 B Sternfels and D Pacthod, "The CEO as elite athlete: What business leaders can learn from modern sports", *McKinsey & Company*, 30 January 2025, www.mckinsey.com/capabilities/strategy-and-corporate-finance/our-insights/the-ceo-as-elite-athlete-what-business-leaders-can-learn-from-modern-sports.

16 SG Carmichael, "How an Olympic gold medalist learned to perform under pressure", *Harvard Business Review*, 12 February 2014, https://hbr.org/2014/02/how-an-olympic-gold-medalist-learned-to-perform-under-pressure.

17 AC Edmondson, *Right Kind of Wrong: The Science of Failing Well* (Atria Books, 2023).

18 J Strauss (director) and T Lee (producer), *Full Measure: The Steve Gladstone Story* [Film] (TXL Adventure Productions, 2023), www.fullmeasurethefilm.com/.

19 T Roosevelt, "Address at the Sorbonne in Paris, France: 'Citizenship in a Republic'", 23 April 1910; GP and JT Woolley, *The American Presidency Project*, www.presidency.ucsb.edu/documents/address-the-sorbonne-paris-france-citizenship-republic.

20 J Collins, *Good to Great: Why Some Companies Make the Lean ... and Others Don't* (Random House Business, 2001).

21 B Horowitz, *The Hard Thing About Hard Things: Building a Business When There Are No Easy Answers* (Harper Business, 2014).

22 ME Porter, "The Five Competitive Forces That Shape Strategy", *Harvard Business Review* 86(1), January 2008, 78–93, https://hbr.org/2008/01/the-five-competitive-forces-that-shape-strategy.

23 F Vermeulen, "Stop Comparing Management to Sports", *Harvard Business Review*, June 2016, https://hbr.org/2016/06/stop-comparing-management-to-sports.

24 T Lasn, "A Company is Not a Family. It's a Sports Team", TrevorLasn.com, 4 October 2024, www.trevorlasn.com/blog/a-company-is-not-a-family-its-a-sports-team.

25 H Inoue and Y-Y Liu, "Revealing the intricate effect of collaboration on innovation," arXiv, 2013, https://arxiv.org/abs/1309.2797.

V. Family matters: advising families on reputation and privacy in the age of AI

James Hann
Digitalis

1. Introduction

The technological landscape that we are navigating today is largely unrecognisable from that of the late 2000s, when the phrase 'artificial intelligence' (AI) was unspoken among advisers and Google alone was the basis of an individual's reputation. I joined Digitalis in 2018 after eight years of service in the British Army and I am now approaching the point at which my time working with private clients tallies with my time as a soldier. As is true in warfare, some advice will never become outdated, but much requires constant refreshing. The advice on how information is obtained, shared, processed, disseminated and, above all, influenced is rapidly changing as we adjust to the 'new normal'.

This 'new normal' means realising not only that many of us have large digital footprints with significant volumes of personal and private data out there online, but also that the same information is now being actively hoovered up and processed *en masse*. What we have collectively been uploading to the Internet for 20 years has already been scoured, analysed and catalogued as 'training data' for hungry, machine-learning algorithms – algorithms that by design are not interested in the truth, that do not have our best interests at heart and whose inner workings are almost totally hidden from us.

Technology advisers have had to respond swiftly to this new reality in order to understand the methodologies that these algorithms employ and how they might weaponise publicly available information. While there is still a need to know how an interested person can identify clients' digital footprints, there is a greater need to understand how large language models (LLMs) and other generative AI technologies are replicating these steps so that we can accurately and effectively advise clients on how to improve their privacy and positively influence their profiles.

As with any new technological development, there are some opportunities to be had, but also many risks. The most immediate departure from traditional advice pertains to the desire of many families to remain hidden from public scrutiny. Ten years ago, it might still have been possible to advise a family on realistic steps to keep their digital profile to an absolute minimum or on strategies to avoid having any meaningful kind of public profile at all. This approach of avoiding any online engagement is now deeply flawed given the very real tendency of LLMs to choose either the first relevant source available (regardless of the veracity or perspective) or simply to create entirely fictitious information when asked about them.

Understanding the changing technology landscape and how it affects wealthy families and the ways in which they are advised is now more important than ever. This chapter focuses on how families can adapt to the changing times and what practical steps are available to improve their privacy and profiles.

2. The challenges facing families

Families face a unique set of challenges to maintain their privacy and protect their reputation, including cyberattacks, privacy concerns leaked financial documents, scrutiny of offshore structures and a continued public agenda against wealth. All of these risks can be exacerbated by the availability of sensitive information across the public domain.

Members of a family spanning generations will have varying levels of technical understanding and appreciations of privacy. It is common to find a family in which the senior generation has a strong appreciation of privacy but a limited technical understanding, while the younger generation that is destined to succeed has a much more developed technical understanding of the digital landscape, but a relatively limited appreciation of digital privacy. This is usually as a result of the next generation's early adoption of technology and the senior generation's general distrust and limited daily usage of digital platforms and tools. In addition, it is common for different generations (and individuals within a generation) to have digital footprints that vary greatly in size, with younger generations often more inclined to

Understanding the changing technology landscape and how it affects wealthy families and the ways in which they are advised is now more important than ever.

overshare personal and familial details online. The differences in information engagement and consumption habits will also present challenges that vary across a single family.

These are, of course, generalisations; however, they are remarkably consistent across high-net-worth, multi-generational families and technology advisers need to bridge the gap between opposing positions within the same family. We do this by understanding the objectives and requirements of a family and where the various members are in terms of digital exposure; and by developing common strategies that all members can stick to.

When it comes to reputation and privacy, a family is only as strong as its weakest link. A unified digital strategy, adhered to by all members, is a critical component of protecting the family's reputation and remaining in control of the narrative. It is for this reason that visibility of any issues, whether legacy or current, is one of the most important factors in protecting a family.

Frequently, the first step in this process is an audit of a family's digital footprint, which might include individual members as well as their family offices, businesses, corporate interests and investment vehicles. As detailed above, there are many factors that can present a problem for families should scrutiny of them suddenly increase; as such, it is important to understand not only what private information is available online, but also how it could be weaponised against them. Nuanced analysis of a family's current reputation and any efforts that have been made to date to present a certain picture should be carefully contrasted with what is available online, highlighting information that could be used to portray potential double standards or hypocrisies. For example, we have worked with families that have been in the process of significantly increasing their philanthropic activity while maintaining links to corporate interests that could easily be juxtaposed to cause reputational embarrassment or harm. It is important to clearly understand these risks and plan for them ahead of time, before the family find themselves under the media spotlight.

In addition to understanding any reputational risks, it is imperative that families have a clear sense of any privacy, security and cyber vulnerabilities, all of which are likely to be targeted by hostile parties. Given the media agenda against wealth and the public interest and scrutiny of high-profile families, it is important to specifically address how easily members of a family can be approached by a journalist or fixated individual. Knowing the extent of public information regarding addresses, contact details, vehicles and life patterns enables a comprehensive strategy to be formulated to minimise or mitigate

It is imperative that families have a clear sense of any privacy, security and cyber vulnerabilities, all of which are likely to be targeted by hostile parties.

risks. In many instances, online application forms exist for individuals to request the removal of personal data; and where they do not, discreet legal approaches or polite requests can often yield results in reducing or limiting the visibility of personally identifying information.

In one situation, a family could be tied to a key residential property through an architect's website that, while it did not name the family directly, contained metadata which confirmed the family's ties and enabled subsequent identification through property records. A discreet and courteous approach to the architect resulted in the removal of the information; and additional searches confirmed that there were no further public routes to identifying the property as being tied to the family. Criminal organisations make good use of these vulnerabilities when conducting target reconnaissance and for families living in jurisdictions with a high targeted burglary or kidnap-and-ransom risk, this advice is invaluable. The guidance on these kinds of vulnerabilities is often common sense; however, the vulnerabilities themselves are often overlooked, unless families are aware of them and alive to the potential threat.

In many cases, human error and behaviour are the primary risks. Oversharing of personal information on social media platforms, for example, can lead to the publication of private information or potentially highly reputationally damaging content. There is a fine balance to be struck between privacy and transparency, and families frequently seek assistance with implementing a strategy that does not preclude the usage of social media platforms but that educates members on the ways to maximise privacy from interested parties and to limit data collection and tracking by the platforms themselves. This training is usually targeted at the next generation, who are perhaps part of a wider succession plan, and aims to inculcate a clear understanding of the severe risks posed by oversharing on social media. This training, like reputation management generally, requires a diplomatic and sensitive approach and close collaboration with families and their advisers to ensure that advice can be easily adopted.

3. Changing technology

AI and generative technologies have transformed the nature of technology advisers' relationships with families and other clients more than any other technological development in the last decade. There are, no doubt, many areas of change yet to be realised, but a number of specific issues have arisen as a result of the availability and implementation of LLMs and other content generation tools.

Largely, these issues can be boiled down to the ever-increasing ease of content generation and the ability to create passable content that can be used to attack families or spread harmful or misleading narratives.

In addition, the method through which LLMs select sources when building responses has led to the inclusion of problematic or outright false information which can cause significant confusion and reputational damage. The issues discussed below in this section can affect any individual and serve to highlight some of the more egregious examples of where technology is letting us down. Potential recourse options can vary from simple measures that individuals can implement themselves to more complex multilateral approaches involving legal and communications experts.

3.1 The vacuum effect

Before the mass adoption of LLMs and before the introduction of AI 'overviews', an individual's online reputation hinged on the top 10 results for their name on a given search engine. Until the mass adoption of ChatGPT (and other leading chatbots), Google accounted for over 90% of the client profiles we worked on; amazingly, Bing is steadily climbing in relevance for clients due to ChatGPT's underlying reliance (not sole but predominant) on results stemming from its index.

On search engines, the factors used to determine the placement of URLs in the rankings are constantly shifting, being updated, rolled out or removed. However, it is accepted that a handful of key factors largely determine where and how a webpage might rank for a keyword. These include quality content, backlinks, keyword optimisation, user experience, click-through rates and technical optimisation factors (eg, site speed, mobile-friendliness, crawlability by the search engine). There are many other elements that influence this, but these are reliably understood to be core to the 'performance' of a given URL in relation to a keyword. This means that between these factors, there is a reasonably good chance that information ranking for an individual's name is relevant (even if it might be considered by them to be problematic). If an individual has a relatively limited profile and few relevant webpages about them, a search results page will very likely contain either namesakes or irrelevant results. In understanding the search journey conducted by a researcher, we know that fewer than 1% of users click through to the second page – meaning that a user's mind will be made up having scanned the (likely) top 10 results, opened a few, made decisions and come to a determination. For highly private individuals, this lack of relevant results translates into inaccurate responses when chatbots are asked to provide answers to questions about them. Most chatbots appear to be quite shallow in their source selection, meaning that they will often select the first apparently relevant result. The inaccuracies which can result range from funny and benign mistakes to massively problematic reputational issues.

The damage being done to critical thinking skills by the mass adoption of generative AI tools means that the window to conduct a critical assessment is closing fast.

Where limited information exists, we see a clear pattern of chatbots attempting to build detailed answers from any source that they see as relevant, especially if that source ranks prominently in the results for an individual. In one recent example, an individual with a very limited online profile was featured in a mainstream news article as part of a wider story. The article appeared in the search record for their name (ie, ranked on Google) alongside a majority of irrelevant namesake results. The article referred to issues at a business in which the individual had previously worked; and despite there being no confirmation of the individual being in any way tied to these issues (itself acknowledged within the article), various chatbot responses suggested that the individual was directly associated with them. The lack of control over the first page of results is an example of where the 'vacuum effect' comes into play: with no active effort by the individual to control the narrative, the LLMs were compelled to fill the gap.

The damage being done to critical thinking skills by the mass adoption of generative AI tools means that the window to conduct a critical assessment is closing fast. In practice, this means that a given user might take the chatbot response to a query at face value. Worse still, individuals from organisations are training enterprise chatbot models to conduct compliance-based assessments on potential clients as part of onboarding processes. Given what we now know about chatbot hallucinations, there may well be many cases of false determinations made by chatbot algorithms designed to eagerly find an answer – any answer.

What this means in practice for ultra-private families desperate to fly below the radar is that keeping a minimal profile and adopting a hands-off approach to online reputation management are no longer options. The chatbots will simply create a profile and response for them, errors and all.

3.2 Shallow source selection

Another area of concern is that of sourcing – namely, how LLMs select sources and how they cite information within their responses. The technology is largely 'black box', meaning that we have no insight into precisely how the algorithms that they employ work or what factors might be contributing to one URL being selected as a source over others. We have been conducting a research programme into widely used chatbots in an attempt to gain a clearer understanding of how they select sources. The findings indicate that on average (across multiple subject categories, queries and chatbots), over 50% of sources selected were either owned assets (eg, webpages, owned biographies, profiles) or Wikipedia articles. In addition, more than

What this means in practice for ultra-private families desperate to fly below the radar is that keeping a minimal profile and adopting a hands-off approach to online reputation management are no longer options.

60% of the sources selected ranked on the first page of results for the subject keyword (across Google/Bing). This means that factors such as negative sentiment bias (common to search engine and social media algorithms) have a disproportionate effect on chatbot responses, due to negative content frequently having much greater ranking potential. Again, it is easy to see why these factors can cause problems for individuals with limited online profiles.

3.3 Hallucinations and conflations

It is now well understood and accepted that an inherent feature of chatbots is the propensity to 'hallucinate'. While this is a fluid concept, it is generally understood to refer to the phenomenon of LLMs generating factually incorrect, misleading or nonsensical information that isn't supported by underlying sources or training data. Most commonly, hallucinations appear following directional user queries, where a user asks a leading question or prompt resulting in a determined effort by the chatbot to generate a response regardless of the existence or availability of relevant information. In one instance identified during the course of routine digital monitoring, we asked ChatGPT: "Is [client business] involved in any controversies?" In response, ChatGPT claimed that our client was involved in the breakup of a multinational business. When asked for a source to back up this claim, ChatGPT provided us with a link to a *Financial Times* article that it had used. The URL did not work and site command searches for the *Financial Times* on Google revealed there had never been an article referring to the client and the alleged breakup action. When pressed to explain where the *Financial Times* citation had come from, the chatbot stated:

> *I apologise for any confusion earlier. Upon further review, I couldn't find a specific source to support the claim that [client business] was directly involved in the breakup of [company name]. It appears that my previous response may have contained inaccurate information. I appreciate your patience and understanding.*

It took two attempts at drilling into the sourcing to get the model to admit this.

When we conducted digital trawls of the Internet to determine how this hallucination might have come about, we discovered a media article about the breakup of the multinational in which a passing reference was made to our client's involvement in the same industry (not in relation to the multinational itself). The risk of conflation can present serious reputational challenges – not least because many hallucinated responses are unknown until targeted searches reveal them.

In situations where a family or business has found itself in a dispute or narrative battle, attempts may be made to seed hostile information into chatbot outputs. If a subject (individual or company) has a limited online footprint, adversaries may seek to place a problematic blog or website high in the rankings. If such a website – which will often contain problematic or defamatory content – is sufficiently well optimised for an individual's name, there is a good chance that it will rank highly. If the chatbots see this ranking in the top half of the first page (and don't distinguish the sentiment to determine that it is hostile to the individual), it might well be used to form the basis of detailed responses to user queries.

3.4 Generated hostile content

One significant impact of generative artificial technology is the way in which it facilitates the creation and weaponisation of hostile content, especially in anonymous defamatory attacks against individuals. The Internet has always enabled anonymous attacks and harassment; however, the ease with which a hostile party can now execute every stage of a sophisticated campaign against someone has led to a significant increase in the number of cases in the private and corporate space. The techniques and operational procedures at play today were previously the purview of state-sponsored or other highly sophisticated actors only. Everything from sock-puppet account creation, reCAPTCHA bypassing, generated adversarial network image generation, content creation and even promotion and amplification techniques is now readily facilitated through the use of generative technologies. We have worked on a number of projects for families caught up in sophisticated attempts to smear them through the waging of a disinformation campaign.

In one sensitive matter in 2024, a client was the victim of a smear campaign that took the form of synthetic pay-to-publish articles on spurious 'media' websites, as well as an orchestrated social media campaign launched on X. The family had instigated legal action against a company which had defrauded their family office through an investment scheme. During the course of proceedings, the campaign hit the client and resulted in significant reputational harm and embarrassment at having to explain the situation to existing investment positions. Some small silver linings and learnings are emerging from these situations, however – not least regarding the strategies that are effective in countering this type of activity. In this instance, we were able to demonstrate both the inaccuracies and the falsehoods within the pay-to-publish articles, and to point out that they were highly likely to have been generated by a chatbot. This analysis facilitated the removal of the majority of offending articles and allowed us to create a counter-narrative to allay the concerns of interested parties.

Deepfake technology is developing at pace and while experts are attempting to create counter-technology, the speed and ease with which a deepfake image, video or audio can be created and deployed (and subsequently engaged with at a viral scale) far outpace any efforts to prevent or stop one in its tracks.

The other key category of generated hostile content which can affect all clients is synthetic or manipulated and 'deepfake' content. Deepfake technology is developing at pace and while experts are attempting to create counter-technology, the speed and ease with which a deepfake image, video or audio can be created and deployed (and subsequently engaged with at a viral scale) far outpace any efforts to prevent or stop one in its tracks.

Issues resulting from this technology seem to be arising in two scenarios in particular. The first relates to children at prestigious private schools and education facilities. Like other prominent institutions and organisations, private schools are subject to cyberattacks – frequently in the form of ransomware attacks based on the use of manipulated images. Horrifically, these attacks often target the open social media feeds of young pupils to create child sexual exploitation material, which is then used in an attempt to blackmail the institution into paying a ransom to prevent any reputational fallout.

The second circumstance in which deepfakes are commonly deployed concerns extortion or 'sextortion' attempts – again, frequently targeting younger members of a family who have inadvertently advertised family wealth and therefore made themselves a target for hostile actors. Other examples of deepfake attacks include the capture and synthesising of a family member's voice – often from open video-based social media accounts (eg, TikTok, Instagram) – which is used to train a model to follow a script designed to cause kneejerk reactions when targeted at other family members (eg, parents). In one instance, a high-net-worth client recounted a situation in which she received a phone call from her daughter in significant distress, asking for money to resolve an urgent problem – all while her daughter was sitting in the same room as her.

In most cases, work to support families in this area centres on promoting understanding and sharing advice, mapping exposure and vulnerabilities and presenting a strategy to mitigate and educate. The following section details some of the practical steps that families can take to protect against these threats.

4. Practicalities

While prominent and wealthy families are increasingly vulnerable, there are steps that can be taken to mitigate these risks and, in some cases, remove them entirely. The following 'Five As' lay out a clear framework for private families to follow to better manage their digital footprints.

4.1 Audit

The first step that a family should take on the road to digital privacy is an audit, to understand what information about them, their family and their business is actually out there online. Only by having a clear view of existing vulnerabilities can families begin to put in place additional protective measures. As mentioned, for families with extremely small digital footprints, it is worth considering where and how the digital narrative regarding their family is being formed. Avoiding the vacuum effect is key and it is imperative to establish a discreet but discoverable profile that offers chatbots an easy-to-source and aligned history. We are beginning to understand the sources that chatbots most readily rely on; taking advantage of this knowledge to seed the *right* information is vital.

4.2 Awareness

As is demonstrated in this chapter, the technological landscape is constantly changing and as such, the need to stay up to date with technical knowledge is a priority concern. Families should thus strive to make digital literacy a core part of their culture. Family governance advisers likewise reiterate the importance of ensuring that all members are on the same page with a strategy that works for everyone. Outside of family, wider circles – including friends and staff – should be kept abreast of the issues and risks posed by careless online activity, especially anything which is likely to increase the risk of a family member being targeted by criminals. Regular training on the latest cyber essentials skills is vital, including recent or trending scams, known vulnerabilities and entry points of attack. Finally, next-generation training on the above themes is highly beneficial, to give the rising members the best chance to succeed and safely manage their own profiles.

4.3 Alerts

It is, of course, possible to use technology to fight technology. Having conducted a baseline assessment of existing vulnerabilities, it is time to think about ways to conduct ongoing monitoring for a family's name, members and business interests – all of which could be targeted and will likely benefit from advanced warning of misuse. Setting up monitoring alerts can range from simple steps that can be implemented by anyone at home to a more comprehensive programme encompassing professional tools designed to look beyond surface web locations.

4.4 Authentication

I recently spent a week in Switzerland visiting trusted family advisers. One thing that was repeatedly stressed was the trend towards in-person, face-to-face authentication of transactions. One adviser even said that they would seek in-person verification for a $100 transaction

Outside of family, wider circles – including friends and staff – should be kept abreast of the issues and risks posed by careless online activity, especially anything which is likely to increase the risk of a family member being targeted by criminals.

to limit the risk of a small fraudulent payment leading to a greater problem. Codewords and verification through a second channel are two methods used by many families to confirm the veracity of a request. Most importantly, if a request sounds urgent, that is the time to pause and verify before taking any further action. Scammers rely on time pressure to defraud their targets.

4.5 Advisers

We recommend that families build a team of advisers and allies *before* these are needed. Having the right people on board who know how to react in a major situation is essential and precious time can be lost trying to find those people in the middle of a crisis. This team should include lawyers, digital investigators, cyber experts, communications specialists and reputation managers.

5. Final word

The technological landscape is evolving quickly. In many ways, it's moving faster than individual counter-technologies can be developed (deepfakes are the key consideration here). However, increasing awareness of the risks posed by the speed of this development means that families are already doing a lot of what they need to do in order to safeguard their reputations. As the current generation take their place at the table, the gap between their knowledge and that of their forebears seems to be shrinking. Knowledge alone, however, will not keep the threats at bay and those families which successfully keep themselves safe and out of the limelight are those that instil the right attitude, centred on privacy and a healthy dose of paranoia.

VI. Why investment decisions are not only about money: navigating goals and building family consensus

Maya Prabhu
J.P. Morgan Private Bank
Sonya Gladstone
Rhian-Anwen Hamill
RAH Partners

1. Introduction

For wealthy families, the advice on how to invest is abundant. Sometimes, however, the real challenge is navigating what lies beneath investment decisions. For many, wealth is the fruit of their life's work and the decisions made about what to do with it carry commensurate weight. The fundamental consideration – before any investment decisions can be made – is for the family to view that money as a means to an end and, most importantly, to ask themselves: what exactly is that end? What are we trying to achieve?

This is a complex question, entangled with longstanding generational views of how the wealth was created, by whom, how it should be spent or saved, and what it was created to do. For some families, wealth is a means for the family to grow and thrive. For other families, it's a safety net, not to be meddled with; while others still see it as tool for making a positive impact on the world or to help in an area that they are passionate about. Often, it's a combination of these goals. Ultimately, the crucial questions underlying all of the above are: what is the wealth for? And how can it empower the family – both as individuals and as a collective – to achieve their goals?

As family advisers, we have come together to discuss how we advise families to answer these fundamental questions, to underscore the importance of this process and to offer actionable strategies. Above all, we focus on the human elements behind investment decisions.

First, we consider how best to navigate the various dimensions of consensus that have emerged in our work. These include differences in abilities and understanding among family members, varying risk appetites and distinct preferences for control and decision-making processes. We also take into account diverse attitudes towards the allocation of time, generational differences in values, differences between siblings and unique lifestyle needs. By addressing each of these factors thoughtfully, we aim to foster alignment and effective collaboration within the family.

These are just some of the ways in which past patterns can resurface. For each of these common dynamics, we draw on case studies to illustrate real-world examples and offer strategies to help families move forward constructively.

Second, we outline how to begin conversations to create resolution and shift disagreement towards a collective view. This involves anchoring dialogue in family history, restructuring communication and clearly defining the goals and governance frameworks.

Rarely is risk appetite uniform across a family: one family member may equate high-risk investments with recklessness, while another may view a low-risk strategy as a path to stagnation.

Finally, we highlight the nuances advisers must consider, stressing the importance of tailored solutions. Every family's circumstances and needs are unique – advice must be too.

In conclusion, we outline the wide-ranging dynamics that families often face when making investment decisions, emphasising the importance of the human element. Drawing on both our professional experience and insights from the J.P. Morgan Private Bank *2026 Global Family Office Report* – which captured perspectives from 333 family offices worldwide, each with an average net worth of $1.6 billion – we illustrate that significant families are best served when they place the human dimension at the heart of their decision making.[1]

2. Navigating the dimensions of family consensus

2.1 Different abilities and understandings

We begin by exploring the frequently unspoken challenges that families face.

The first difference – and one of the most fundamental – is that family members have varying levels of ability and understanding surrounding investments. Some members may have had a formal education in finance or other relevant areas, while others may bring practical experience with asset allocation, investment management or macroeconomic skills that contribute to building a diversified portfolio. Others may have neither education nor experience. While this may seem like a simple barrier on the surface, if left unaddressed, a family can risk making members feel isolated or want to withdraw from conversations if they feel that they don't have a voice. This dynamic can be overcome by ensuring that family members have the necessary support and educational resources to make the conversations around investments accessible for all.

2.2 Differing risk appetites

Differing approaches to risk present another hurdle for families trying to reach investment consensus. Each individual's risk appetite is deeply personal and is shaped by a variety of factors. Rarely is risk appetite uniform across a family: one family member may equate high-risk investments with recklessness, while another may view a low-risk strategy as a path to stagnation. These perspectives are often rooted in the origins of the wealth or shaped by life experiences, and can be influenced by personality traits, such as the 'entrepreneurial' versus 'conservative' mindset. Even day-to-day factors such as mood, sleep quality and general optimism regarding the future can affect how family members view risk.

More commonly, individuals' risk appetites follow consistent patterns throughout family conversations. You may encounter one family member who is more entrepreneurial – someone who enjoys taking risks and is daring with capital. Perhaps they have experienced success with a risky investment; or perhaps their entrepreneurial spirit simply drives them to build the capital in a way that others may consider to be too speculative. Conversely, another family member may be more conservative: their goal is to safely build the capital, preferring a steadier growth trajectory; and they are not enthused by the possibility of larger, riskier payoffs, as the potential downsides are not worth it to them. This creates a spectrum of behaviour within the family.

We often see families establish a primary collective pot to achieve their broader wealth goals, which can be further divided into specialised 'sleeves' dedicated to preservation, growth and impact. Alongside this collective pot, families may allocate smaller, individual pots to each member, granting them full autonomy over their own finances. This approach encourages personal exploration – giving one member the freedom to invest in impact projects while another focuses on real estate or emerging technologies such as e-sports. For this strategy to succeed, it must be implemented thoughtfully. Providing the necessary financial education and professional advice is essential to ensure that individuals are equipped to manage this independence responsibly. To use a food analogy: the collective pot ensures that the meal is balanced, while the individual pots allow everyone to choose their own flavour, respecting personal values and autonomy.

Sometimes, families worry that family members may lose all the money in their personal pots and wonder how best to address this concern. In our experience, there are multiple effective strategies and each family should consider what is most appropriate based on factors such as financial knowledge, reliance on the funds and whether the pot is designed to be 'experimental' or to support a family member's living expenses. Often, when there are significant differences in financial understanding, families establish a unified investment policy to ensure that no one is exposed to undue risk.

2.3 Engagement

The next common factor at play when working to build consensus is varying levels of engagement among family members. Individuals often have diverse perceptions of what it means to be engaged in investment decisions. This is frequently evident in the contrast between 'on the pitch' and 'spectator' dynamics: one family member may believe that their investment decisions should carry more weight due to their daily involvement in the business and operational oversight, while another may prefer a more detached, observational role.

The varying levels of engagement of each family member can shape the family's *modus operandi* and can significantly influence investment decisions. When the family decision-making process is based on informal dynamics rather than a structured framework, tensions can arise. We observed this firsthand in a case where a previously disengaged family member attempted to intervene, disrupting established routines and causing friction with those who had remained actively involved. Such power struggles, often rooted in the broader family history, can cloud investment decisions.

2.4 Allocation of time

Another related factor is the differing allocation of time among family members. A common scenario that we have seen involves two siblings – one of whom spends every day in the family office managing the granular details of the portfolio and another who does not. This dynamic can often create a sense of imbalance, as the more active sibling may feel that their time investment should grant them a greater degree of authority, while the less active sibling still expects their ownership to translate into equal decision-making power. Such situations often lead to mutual resentment, with each judging the other for how they choose to allocate their time.

One effective strategy in these scenarios is to establish a clear process for how decisions are reached, how time is valued and how much influence each family member has. It is important that these processes remain flexible and can be amended as needed. Additionally, providing compensation for time spent can help to address any perceived imbalance of contribution among family members.

2.5 Generational and values divide

Another important dynamic to consider when discussing and understanding the purpose of family wealth is the presence of differing values, both between and within generations. According to the J.P. Morgan Private Bank *2026 Global Family Office Report*, nearly six in 10 global family offices identified the preservation of family values, governance and legacy as a top priority.[2] As families expand and generations multiply, maintaining a shared vision and guiding principles becomes increasingly complex. The further a family is from its founding generation, the more acute these challenges become. In fact, the survey found that families tend to adopt more formal governance measures as they grow across generations, reflecting their increasing complexity and evolving needs.

While older generations often prioritise the practical realities of traditional sectors and immediate, positive cash flow, younger members may advocate for stronger alignment with environmental, social and governance principles as well as exposure to emerging

Is family capital fundamentally a multi-generational legacy to be preserved or should it be actively redistributed through philanthropy and tax?

frontiers such as Web3 or space technology. This friction is not limited to the parent-child dynamic; even among siblings, perspectives can diverge sharply.

Beyond asset allocation, these conversations often bring deeper philosophical questions about the nature and purpose of wealth to the forefront. Is family capital fundamentally a multi-generational legacy to be preserved or should it be actively redistributed through philanthropy and tax? In an era defined by extreme wealth inequality and the rise of movements such as the Patriotic Millionaires, younger generations may experience a sense of shame or visibility regarding their privilege. This guilt, often felt most acutely by those who did not create the original fortune, can lead to difficult conversations.

Whether the focus is on clean water, gender equity or sustainable governance, the push for impact investing reflects a desire to align personal values with investment decisions. Addressing the embarrassment or guilt associated with inequality requires a shift in the family conversation. Without a willingness to learn and grow together, families risk allowing these differences in values to become barriers to consensus.

This friction is frequently compounded by a mismatch in engagement levels and personal agendas. Family members who are deeply interested in the technicalities of finance may feel a sense of resentment towards family members who are disengaged yet still hold an equal vote on major decisions.

2.6 Lifestyle needs

Furthermore, individual capital needs rarely align perfectly and lifestyle requirements can vary significantly among family members. Luxury for one family member may be considered normalcy for another. Where family members choose to have their main homestead can also result in drastically different lifestyle needs, influenced by factors such as the cost of living, tax structures in different countries and many other variables.

Family members may also hold differing perspectives on the purpose of family wealth. One member might view the family wealth as a vital safety net for the core operating business; another could see it primarily as a source of lifestyle funding; while a third may be advocating for aggressive growth to build their own independent legacy. Investment discussions are often weighed down with these competing priorities, turning what should be a straightforward financial exercise into a complex navigation of family dynamics and psychology.

2.7 Managing historical family dynamics

The factors discussed thus far in this chapter have a common thread: investment conversations often serve as an unintended forum for surfacing long-entrenched family roles, airing past grievances and replaying dynamics. When discussing current portfolios, it is common for members to backslide into their historical roles – such as 'the controlling patriarch', 'the dismissive sibling' or the 'caring peacemaker' – regardless of their actual professional expertise. These ingrained patterns can easily overshadow the financial planning process, giving precedence to underlying power dynamics between the people in the room. When these emotional histories lead, a financial opinion or critique can be interpreted as a personal slight rooted in decades of history, making objective consensus almost impossible.

3. Creating resolution through shifting conversations

To move from these entrenched dynamics towards consensus, families can begin by shifting the focus of conversations away from investment decisions and towards the human issues that underpin them. Resolution is rarely about one side winning out over another; instead, it is about establishing a dialogue that allows for multiple perspectives, processes and ways of operating that fit within the broader family goals. This process begins by anchoring the family to a long-term purpose, reflecting on their shared history and the achievements that they are most proud of, while also honestly examining the elements they now question – whether related to specific industries, tax structures or outdated working practices.

In this section, we outline three essential strategies for restructuring the dialogue around investment decisions:

- Anchor conversations in family history to move beyond old patterns and foster understanding of differing perspectives.
- Restructure discussions away from emotional responses and encourage more objective, fact-based dialogue.
- Define goals and governance frameworks to ensure competence and promote shared impact.

By placing shared values and a sense of purpose at the heart of every decision and maintaining a forward-looking approach, the family can move beyond old conflicts or different ways of operating and create a sense of purpose and cohesion – both personally and in terms of their investments, their philanthropy and any operating businesses. Conversations that focus on values and purpose, and discussions of the ends to which the family feels their wealth provides the means, can help the family to move towards a unified strategy that is both focused and sustainable.

Conversations that focus on values and purpose, and discussions of the ends to which the family feels their wealth provides the means, can help the family to move towards a unified strategy that is both focused and sustainable.

3.1 Anchoring dialogue in history

One powerful tool for building family cohesion is the process of revisiting family history. When family members share their personal experiences of key milestones, it fosters empathy and helps the family to find restorative common ground. Looking back is often a way to effectively look forward: it allows the group to identify patterns that have historically dictated their financial behaviour.

To illustrate this dynamic, we can examine one family that we worked with where one member realised that their history was defined by a cycle of making money and then reacting out of insecurity, buying at market peaks and selling at the bottom during downturns or periods of geographic relocation. By reviewing their family events together and acknowledging their individual interpretations of these, they could finally begin to understand this cycle. Collectively, they decided that the one thing they did not want to pass on to the third generation was this sense of insecurity. Their new mission became the active pursuit of 'securing' the wealth and breaking the cycle of reactive decision making.

Anchoring conversations in family history can also help members to understand their unique communication style. Families often have distinct communication cultures: some may prefer a more harmonious, indirect approach to sensitive topics, while others embrace a rigorous, debate-driven style. Some may rely heavily on outside advisers to facilitate, while others maintain a traditional structure centred around a lead figure. By recognising these inherent dynamics before high-stakes conversations occur, families can proactively adjust their approach. This ensures that the dialogue remains a constructive exchange that fosters mutual understanding, leading to more open and collaborative conversations in the future.

3.2 Restructuring communication

Once families have developed a better understanding of their differing views of family history, they can consciously restructure the way in which they communicate. As advisers, we have found that beginning with the objective of shifting members away from emotional responses and towards factual processing is often a useful tool. This can be achieved by implementing 'emotional learning' guidelines, such as the practice of listening specifically in order to understand rather than simply to formulate a rebuttal. By allowing each member to share their perspective without interruption, the family can evolve in their communications. This structured approach ensures that every voice is heard, which reduces the likelihood of members feeling sidelined and prevents the conversation from devolving into a series of defensive exchanges. Further, it creates a safe space to acknowledge how past behaviours may be influencing current discussions, allowing the group to move beyond emotional issues that are impacting the conversation.

In fact, the J.P. Morgan Private Bank *2026 Global Family Office Report* found that regular family gatherings – such as meetings, assemblies and retreats – are among the most common approaches to fostering cohesion and alignment, with nearly half of family offices adopting these practices.[3] As families expand across generations, evolving from a single parental unit into multiple branches and geographically dispersed households, the importance of formal engagement initiatives grows. These initiatives extend beyond traditional gatherings, encompassing structured family oversight, the formalisation of shared values and mission, the preservation of legacy and the development of a unified financial infrastructure.

3.3 Defining governance and goals

The third key to overcoming the barriers to consensus and promoting positive, productive communication is to clearly define the goals and governance structures of the wealth.

One case study of governance comes from our work with a family that uses the 'pot' or 'bucket' approach, where assets are categorised according to their specific purpose. Once the family understands how the various 'buckets' are allocated, the next step is the codification of an 'investment policy statement', which is read, understood and agreed

Education is vital as it creates a shared language that enables everyone to ask informed questions during meetings. This significantly reduces feelings of disenfranchisement or entitlement and ensures that investments remain anchored to the family's collective mission.

upon by every family member. This document serves as the family's financial constitution, defining strategic asset allocation, target returns and specific parameters for investments.

To execute this, two governance processes are often established. First, the most successful families invest in establishing a baseline of financial literacy for all members. This may involve formal training through an academic institution or bespoke guidance tailored to the family's specific needs. Education is vital as it creates a shared language that enables everyone to ask informed questions during meetings. This significantly reduces feelings of disenfranchisement or entitlement and ensures that investments remain anchored to the family's collective mission.

The second process involves establishing an investment committee to bridge the gap between high-level vision and day-to-day management. The J.P. Morgan Private Bank *2026 Global Family Office Report* found that 83% of family offices globally have some degree of formal governance in place, with investment committees being the most common structure.[4] This committee typically includes a lead family member or the head of the family office, as well as external experts such as a bank representative or an outside non-executive director to provide a broader intellectual perspective and challenge when needed. By delegating routine decision making to this group, the family ensures that investments remain strictly anchored to the mission and the designated buckets. The committee then reports back to the wider family once or twice a year, maintaining transparency and collective involvement, without requiring every member to navigate the complexities of daily market movements.

By integrating these key shifts – anchoring in family history, shifting communication and defining goals and governance – families can move towards consensus.

4. Key elements of implementation

Implementing the changes outlined above is rarely a linear process. For the advisers guiding families through this shift, the journey presents unique challenges. In this final section, we examine the common pitfalls for advisers and explain why there is no such thing as a 'template solution' when it comes to navigating the human elements of family investment.

4.1 Nuances for advisers

For advisers, successfully navigating these dynamics requires a deep understanding of the family's culture and the underlying principles that shape their hierarchy, especially when facilitating conversations such as those outlined in this chapter.

For example, the high degree of reverence held for elders in some Middle Eastern and Asian families may mean that consensus is reached through private consultation rather than open dissent in a formal setting. These cultural frameworks are not 'obstacles' to be corrected, but realities that require advisers to remain flexible and adapt their approach accordingly.

Advisers should recognise that the most significant breakthroughs often happen 'off deck', during quiet reflections or private conversations, rather than within the formal agenda. Strict adherence to a pre-set plan can be counterproductive; if the energy in the room shifts or a key member signals the need for a pause, the adviser must be flexible enough to pivot and address the emotional landscape of the room, ensuring that signs such as these are not overlooked in favour of sticking to an agenda.

Because family dynamics are live, unexpected issues can surface as the process unfolds. The most effective advisers act less like lecturers and more as facilitators, prepared to help untangle complex grievances in private, away from the pressure of an open forum, if this is where the family works most productively. This is why it is vital to start each day by asking for reflections on the previous session. This practice serves as a pressure valve, allowing family members to voice concerns or share shifts in perspective that may have emerged overnight.

4.2 No template solutions

Beyond cultural nuance, there is a saying among those who work in family enterprises that goes: "Once you've seen one family office you've seen one family office." The truth of this statement is vital. There are no template solutions for families. While structured frameworks such as 'investment buckets' provide a strong foundation, they must be applied based on the specific personalities involved. A common critique from investment specialists is that fragmenting capital into separate pools is not appropriate for all families. For example, if a family is dealing with a next generation who may be unable to effectively manage their allocation, a 'pot' approach could be disastrous. In such cases, the governance could be more protective and restrictive.

Ultimately, every strategy is situation dependent. What works for a family with high levels of trust and financial literacy may not be effective for a family that is struggling with dysfunction. Advisers cannot hand over a pre-packaged governance model and expect it to succeed. The 'correct' solution only emerges after the adviser has accurately assessed the family's specific risk profiles, cultural backgrounds and individual capabilities. Moving from a generic template to a bespoke reality is essential to ensure that the wealth

By shifting the focus away from the binary question of "Which asset?" and towards the more fundamental question of "To what end?", families can move past the more challenging dimensions of these conversations and find consensus.

serves as a tool for family cohesion, rather than a catalyst for its dissolution.

5. Conclusion

Successful family investing depends on understanding the individuals behind the investment decisions and how their perspectives interact within the broader family system, with all its underlying currents and shifting human dynamics. As we have explored, effective family investing is a function of successful communication and the establishment of governance processes for decision making and sharing information. By shifting the focus away from the binary question of "Which asset?" and towards the more fundamental question of "To what end?", families can move past the more challenging dimensions of these conversations and find consensus. Engaging in values-based discussions before beginning an investment review ensures that wealth is viewed as a means to achieve a collective purpose rather than a source of individual contention.

A strategy lacks a solid foundation if it is not anchored in the family's long-term history. Building consensus requires profound, wide-ranging conversations conducted in a positive communication style, supported by a robust governance framework. However, as our experience across different dynamics has shown, there is no one-size-fits-all template for creating consensus. Every family is a unique ecosystem that demands its own approach. Advisers must remain agile, focusing on the individuals as they are in that present moment rather than relying on pre-packaged models.

By prioritising the human element, families can overcome many barriers. When the underlying 'why' is clearly defined and the communication channels are open, investment decisions become the practical tools used to build a thriving and purposeful family.

Notes

1 J.P. Morgan Private Bank, *2026 Global Family Office Report*, https://assets.jpmprivatebank.com/content/dam/jpm-pb-aem/global/en/documents/2026-family-office-report/jp-morgan-private-bank-2026-global-family-office-report.pdf.
2 *Ibid.*
3 *Ibid.*
4 *Ibid.*

VII. Investment best practice in family offices

Samuel Lawson
Samuel Shaw
Sally Tennant
Acorn Capital Advisers

1. Introduction: capital is abundant, capability is not

> *Be clear early: are you spending 50 or 75 basis points? Build accordingly. Do not back a team you cannot justify. Breadth without depth is an expensive way to get mediocre results.*

Achieving investment best practice for single-family offices is rooted in hiring and empowering the right chief investment officer (CIO), designing a purpose-built investment engine and embedding truly independent voices into governance. However, we have seen a common pattern – especially in first-generation single family offices – of prioritising investments without clarity of purpose and objectives and underinvesting in the talent and governance required to execute effectively. The missing ingredient is rarely opportunity; it is the environment in which decisions are made.

Family office decision making is fundamentally different from institutional models. Regardless of how collaborative the process might be, ultimate authority usually rests with the principal or a small circle of family members. It is their capital, their risk and their legacy. Investment decisions are therefore shaped not just by analysis, but by values, personalities, relationships and intergenerational perspectives. This can be a source of strength, allowing for agility, conviction and long-term thinking; but also of vulnerability, where emotion or politics overrides disciplined investment judgement.

Best practice in family offices is not about replicating institutional processes but about implementing frameworks that enable professional decision making while respecting the family's unique priorities and culture. In this chapter, we explore this through three interconnected pillars.

1.1 Pillar I: The role of the CIO

The CIO is the captain of the investment capability, responsible for strategy, execution and alignment with the family's values and governance. But in a family office, investment skill alone is not enough. The most effective CIOs pair market expertise with diplomacy and emotional intelligence, acting as both architect and adviser.

The role is often difficult. Objectives may be unclear, resources lean and decision-making authority blurred by *ad hoc* interventions. The best CIOs operate within a clearly defined mandate, with appropriate resources and governance. They become stewards of the decision-making process, balancing agility with discipline and short-term opportunity with long-term strategy.

1.2 Pillar II: Building and structuring the investment engine

There is no 'one size fits all' model. An effective investment engine is intentionally designed, right-sized to the family's ambition, resources and culture. The strongest offices begin by defining clear objectives and then building the right blend of in-house capability and external partners to deliver on them.

Governance protects the process without creating bureaucracy. Liquidity is actively managed. Multiple objectives – financial, strategic and philanthropic – are integrated into a coherent framework to avoid fragmentation and misalignment. The result is an investment engine that enables good decision making.

1.3 Pillar III: The value of independent voices

Independent advisers bring discipline, healthy challenge and perspective. When carefully chosen and embedded in governance, they strengthen decisions, support the CIO and signal professionalism to the family and externally. True independence is more than simply being unconflicted; advisers must have the ability to offer insight without being influenced by politics or consensus thinking.

The right expertise, cultural fit and clear mandates are critical. The best independent voices enhance, rather than diminish, the family's priorities and enhance the quality and resilience of decision making.

Drawing on our experience as well as insights from leading family office principals, CIOs and investment committee chairs, this chapter offers a practical guide to building a high-performing investment capability in a family office and explores the relationship between the people, processes and governance that shape decision making and sustainable performance.

2. Pillar I: The complex role of the family office CIO

The CIO in a family office is not just an investor; they are a nexus through which capital, governance and family dynamics converge. On paper, their responsibilities may read like any senior investment role: set investment strategy, oversee implementation, manage risk and report performance. In practice, the job is more textured and far more personal.

2.1 First-generation versus multi-generational family offices

One of the biggest variables shaping the CIO's role is the maturity of the family office itself. There is a distinct difference between a first-generation family office and one that has been operating for decades. First-generation offices are usually founder led, entrepreneurial and fast moving, with light governance and investment approaches shaped by the principal's own experience and convictions. Multi-generational

The CIO in a family office is not just an investor; they are a nexus through which capital, governance and family dynamics converge.

offices tend to be more institutional, with formal governance, deeper internal expertise and fewer family members involved in investment decisions. For the CIO, success lies in aligning style, communication and governance to the different dynamics at play. According to one senior ultra-high-net-worth investment adviser: "Is a family better served by a 32-page weekly bulletin or by a two-sentence note that simply reassures them all is well?"

2.2 Balancing investment acumen with emotional intelligence

In both family offices and wealth management institutions, technical ability is a given. The CIO needs to be proficient in asset allocation, manager selection, portfolio construction and risk management – but in a family office, these skills are only part of the equation. The equally critical and often defining capability is emotional intelligence. One CIO suggested that: "The CIO in a family office must be both a portfolio architect and a trusted adviser. They need to read more than markets; they need to read the room."

They must understand the principal's personality, investment experience, unspoken priorities and sensitivities. While it is important to understand whether the family office aims simply to keep up with the markets or inflation or to generate outsized returns, they must

The best CIOs show humility, knowing when to partner, when to expand awareness and when to lean on others.

also recognise when a decision goes beyond the numbers. This does not mean agreeing to every idea. It means constructing portfolios in a way that aligns with the family's priorities without undermining portfolio discipline. "Disagreeing in a loving way" is how one seasoned CIO described it – the ability to push back without eroding trust or creating defensiveness. Sometimes this involves working with the principal to set limits – for example, using options to allow the principal to express conviction in a sector without jeopardising portfolio balance. Other times, it means steering non-core ideas into positions that are too small to harm outcomes.

The CIO in a family office is often as much a psychologist as an investor. They help the family to understand and make good decisions, presenting clear trade-offs and then living with whatever choice is made. A low ego is critical, as for all family office senior executives. They require the confidence to voice a dissenting opinion and the maturity to accept being overruled without damaging the relationship. The best CIOs show humility, knowing when to partner, when to expand awareness and when to lean on others. Far from weakness, this humility fosters stronger partnerships, broader opportunity sourcing and ultimately superior outcomes.

2.3 Building trust

Applying their emotional intelligence, a CIO must then build trust. As one senior family office managing director explained: "Trust is the currency of the CIO. The most effective people have the principal's trust in either their expertise or their judgement. Ideally both. But at least one."

Without trust, no amount of technical skill will be enough to influence outcomes. Every CIO must develop their approach to managing the principal. Some principals want a sparring partner, others a filter. Some expect frequent updates; others only want to hear when a decision is needed from them. The most effective CIOs develop a rhythm that balances respect for the principal's authority with the responsibility to protect the portfolio from undue risk. That can mean being candid about the trade-offs of a favoured idea or, when resistance is high, finding a way to minimise its potential downside without direct confrontation.

Recruitment failures often stem from two issues. The first is when the principal appoints a successful investment banker, private equity professional or trusted private banker to become the CEO/CIO. Few of these professionals have the breadth and depth of experience to construct and oversee a multi-asset class portfolio if that is the core investment strategy. If the strategy centres on private deals, a private equity or banking background may be good fit. Conversely, a principal with a private market-oriented background as a founder might choose someone with a strong understanding of public markets.

Families that approach CIO recruitment as if they were hiring for an institutional role – focusing solely on pedigree, qualifications and track record – can make costly mistakes. A CIO's success depends on more than investment capability. They need to be comfortable working in a discreet, often low-profile environment, thriving without the infrastructure of a large institution and navigating the sensitivities of family dynamics.

2.4 Operating in a family office environment

A family office CIO operates in a fundamentally different environment from an institutional counterpart. In asset management, banks, pension funds and endowments, the CIO leads teams, sets broad strategy and often serves as a public investment voice. Their responsibilities involve layers of specialists, marketing and fundraising. In a family office, the role is more personal and direct, as the ultimate decision maker is also the owner, the client and the person whose legacy is at stake. As one highly respected investment committee chair put it: "This is an autocracy, not a democracy."

The CIO often works with lean teams, sometimes as the sole investment professional, and is expected to make high-conviction decisions quickly. The best CIOs are not 'talking heads' but true investors, able to evaluate an opportunity from first principles, perform their own underwriting and assess risks without layers of intermediaries. According to one seasoned CIO: "You do not have 250 analysts hanging around. You rely on your own skill set a lot more and you must be able to get to the core of the investment quickly."

This proximity to decision making is both a privilege and a pressure. The CIO has direct access to the capital and can move quickly without institutional red tape, but they must also navigate decisions that are deeply personal and sometimes emotionally charged. There are fewer buffers between the CIO and the principal and without the right governance guardrails, this can lead to impulsive or overly concentrated bets. If a decision turns out poorly, there is often no committee vote to hide behind.

One of the CIO's biggest challenges is helping the family to resist the pull of 'infotainment investing', where they may be drawn to opportunities that rely solely on compelling narratives or the push of trend or network-driven investments. The CIO must be able to redirect enthusiasm towards opportunities that meet both the family's appetite for engagement and its need for risk-adjusted returns. As one CIO put it: "Families often under-invest in expertise and over-invest in pet ideas."

There is also the reality that not all the facts behind the decision are visible to the team and they need to be comfortable with this. One CIO recounted an investment that was abandoned without clear reason, only to discover later that a personal falling-out had influenced the decision.

One of the freedoms of the family office CIO role is that there are no external clients, no fundraising roadshows and no quarterly pressures from investors. The CIO's sole client is the family. This creates the opportunity to build genuinely long-term portfolios, free from the distortions of short-term performance chasing. But with that freedom comes acute responsibility. Every gain or loss is felt directly. Decisions are remembered and so is the process that led to them. A robust, transparent approach to decision making is not a luxury; it is the CIO's insurance policy.

One unique advantage for family office CIOs is the ability to leverage the family's name and network to gain access to investment opportunities. This can open doors to high-quality private deals, co-investments alongside respected general partners (GPs) and introductions to sector leaders. However, access is a double-edged sword. You can be thrown hundreds of opportunities but the fact

One unique advantage for family office CIOs is the ability to leverage the family's name and network to gain access to investment opportunities.

that a deal is offered because of the family's profile does not make it a good investment. Without a disciplined screening process, due diligence and governance, access can become a trap, draining resources and leading to illiquidity or concentration risk.

2.5 Mandate clarity and alignment

The recurring barrier to CIO effectiveness is a vague or shifting mandate. Too many CIOs operate in a grey zone, unclear about their decision-making authority, unsure when to escalate or second-guessing whether the family wants leadership or simply execution. Without clarity, the CIO risks falling into the trap of excessive deference to the principal (undermining their own value) or overreach (creating political tension) – or, worse, a disenfranchised CIO with disengaged leadership, giving the appearance of control and governance without enforcement of oversight and risk controls.

A well-structured investment mandate should clearly define the CIO's decision-making authority, specifying which decisions the CIO can make independently, which require approval from the investment committee and which must be escalated to the principal. It should also establish clear boundaries, outlining the asset classes, geographies, sectors and deal sizes that fall within or outside the scope of the mandate. In addition to return targets, the mandate should articulate performance expectations in terms of risk, liquidity and alignment with the family's broader objectives. Finally, it must describe the governance interface, detailing how the CIO engages with the family council, board and investment committee to ensure transparency, accountability and strategic alignment.

Clarity here is not bureaucracy; it enables the CIO to operate effectively and act decisively. Defining this upfront does more than clarify roles; it builds the foundation for accountability and speeds up decision making. It also gives the family a framework to evaluate the CIO fairly, reducing the risk of mismatched expectations. As one CIO put it: "It is easier for the family to support a CIO's decisions when they helped to define the rules of engagement."

2.6 Compensation, retention and alignment

Attracting and retaining top investment talent requires alignment of incentives. Yet many families resist offering in-house staff terms that they readily grant external managers. This inconsistency can breed frustration and churn.

The most effective alignment mechanisms blend salary, performance-based bonuses and opportunities for co-investment or carried interest. Co-investment aligns time horizons and encourages true stewardship of capital. The alignment of incentives at Michael Dell's family office has resulted in the CIO becoming a billionaire following years of exceptional returns. Without alignment, there is a risk that CIOs may prioritise their personal career safety over the family's long-term benefit.

2.7 What attracts and deters CIOs?

CIOs are attracted to family offices that offer:

- genuine autonomy in decision making;
- clear and stable governance;
- alignment through co-investment or carried interest;
- the opportunity to work across multiple asset classes and strategies; and
- a coherent mission that goes beyond simply growing the money.

In contrast, they are often deterred by:

- capricious or inconsistent decision making from principals;
- the lack of a clear investment process;
- limited influence over strategic direction; and
- excessive restrictions on external engagement that constrain their professional profile.

2.8 The CIO is the cultural anchor

Finally, the CIO shapes the culture of the investment function. They set the tone for how opportunities are assessed, how dissent is handled and how decisions are documented. Their approach to risk, communication and collaboration sets the tone for how investment matters are handled within the family. In the best-run family offices, the CIO is not just a manager of capital but a steward of the decision-making process itself. They balance agility with discipline, personal relationships with professional judgement and the opportunities of today with the needs of tomorrow. In some offices, the CIO also plays a key role in engaging the next generation, demystifying the investment process, providing education on investment principles and gradually integrating them into governance roles.

In short, the CIO role in a family office is about more than managing money. It is about building and sustaining the capability to make consistently sound investment decisions in an environment where personal relationships and financial objectives are deeply intertwined. Supported by a clear mandate, robust governance and the right resources, the CIO can turn the family's capital into a resilient, purpose-aligned investment capability that endures through generations.

3. Pillar II: Building and structuring the investment engine

Even the most able CIO cannot succeed in a vacuum. The investment engine – the people, processes, governance and resourcing that support the role – enables strategy to be implemented. In a family office, building that function is not about copying the operating model of a pension fund or endowment. It is about creating something that is right-sized, intentional and adaptable to the family's priorities, scale and culture. A well-designed investment engine makes good decisions easier to reach and harder to derail. A poorly designed one creates bottlenecks, blurs accountability and allows critical risks to go unrecognised or unmitigated. The difference often comes down to whether the family has designed its structure around its strategy or simply allowed it to evolve by default.

3.1 Start with purpose, not structure

The starting point is not "Which roles do we need in the family office?" but rather "What are we actually trying to achieve?" Is the primary objective preserving wealth or compounding it? Or is it finding a new family entrepreneurial business or pursuing a philanthropic impact goal? Will the focus be on liquid markets, alternative funds or direct investments? What is the appetite for illiquidity?

Ultimately, the best family offices match their ambition with adequate resourcing. That does not mean building a sprawling in-house team.

Without clarity of purpose, families risk overbuilding (creating layers of complexity that they do not need), underbuilding (leaving the CIO without the tools to deliver on the mandate) or overdiversifying ('spraying and praying').

3.2 Resourcing decisions: in-house, outsourced or hybrid

After defining the purpose and objectives, the family should begin to consider investment operating models and resourcing: what to keep in-house, what to outsource and what to avoid altogether. In-house control is most valuable where nuanced oversight and family context matter – for example, in setting strategy, managing asset allocation and building long-term relationships with key partners.

Resourcing decisions must be deliberate. This means deciding upfront what you are prepared to spend on your investment function and aligning ambition to that budget. According to one well-respected family office leader: "Be clear early: are you spending 50 or 75 basis points? Build accordingly. Do not back a team you cannot justify. Breadth without depth is an expensive way to get mediocre results."

Teams should be designed around what the family wants to do, not what a generic best-practice template suggests. If the family's passion is direct mid-market private equity co-investment in a specialist area – for example, renewables – it makes sense to build capability there and outsource the rest. If the goal is steady, low-drama capital preservation, the team might focus on asset allocation, manager oversight and liquidity management, with minimal in-house investment resources.

The most common approach is a hybrid model with lean internal leadership supported by targeted external partnerships. Hybrid models sometimes fail in implementation, *ad hoc* outsourcing, unclear responsibilities and duplication – which creates risk. A bespoke platform should define exactly who is responsible for what, how information flows and where accountability sits.

Ultimately, the best family offices match their ambition with adequate resourcing. That does not mean building a sprawling in-house team. Family offices can leverage external partners for tasks including manager research, operational due diligence or specialist sector insight, leaving the CIO with the time to focus on investment strategy.

3.3 Technology as an enabler

In today's vast and complex investment landscape, family offices cannot ignore technology. It is not about owning the latest tools for their own sake, but about deploying technology to manage scale, complexity and efficiency.

Internally, the investment team need systems to track multiple positions across asset classes. The lack of comparability and audit trails is a major weakness. Too often, CIOs cannot fully explain why they made a decision or whether the circumstances at the time still hold. Better systems for learning from past decisions are essential to building resilience and credibility. Externally, they need awareness of how technology itself impacts markets and portfolios.

This extends towards knowing when they place the family at risk too. For family offices, cybersecurity is no longer a back-office issue but a frontline strategic priority. The same digital transformation that delivers opportunities for data-driven insights, operational efficiency and faster decision making also introduces vulnerabilities. As economies digitise and malicious actors deploy ever more sophisticated tactics, the attack surface expands. For a CIO, therefore, vigilance in this area is not optional but a fiduciary responsibility to protect capital, reputation and business continuity. Awareness cannot be a one-off exercise; it requires constant monitoring, testing and adaptation as threats evolve.

3.4 Governance that fits the family

Governance in the investment function must be proportionate to the family's structural complexity and activity level. Too little governance leaves the CIO exposed to *ad hoc* interference and the family exposed to potential reputational and financial risk. Too much governance creates process fatigue and slows decision making unnecessarily. There is a temptation in some family offices to adopt governance and process frameworks borrowed wholesale from institutional investors. While they may look impressive, these structures can quickly become overengineered for the scale and pace of a family office.

Liquidity management is often treated as an operational task when it should be a governance priority. Illiquid investments, especially direct deals, can quietly build to a level that constrains flexibility. Best practice includes a rolling liquidity forecast, explicit minimum liquidity thresholds and a formal process for assessing the impact of new illiquid commitments on the whole portfolio. This ensures that exciting opportunities do not quietly erode the family's ability to respond to unforeseen needs or market shifts.

The most effective investment engines are bespoke, always aligned with the family's real decision-making needs. Governance should be a tool for clarity and execution, not a performance in best practice for its own sake. This gives the investment committee the authority and space to focus solely on investment matters, slightly apart from the broader family council or board, allowing for objective, timely decision making while still reporting into the wider governance structure.

There is a temptation in some family offices to adopt governance and process frameworks borrowed wholesale from institutional investors. While they may look impressive, these structures can quickly become overengineered for the scale and pace of a family office.

Crucially, the role of the family in governance needs clarity. Family members on investment committees risk blurring ownership and management. Better models provide input and visibility without decision rights. That responsibility rests with those who have both the mandate and the expertise to exercise it.

3.5 Structuring for multiple objectives without fragmentation

Today, many families pursue more than just financial return; they have philanthropic and impact objectives or strategic goals that sit alongside the investment portfolio. The risk is that each objective develops its own governance and process, leading to fragmented decision making and uncoordinated capital allocation.

Stronger models unify objectives under one capital allocation process, making trade-offs visible, synergies clearer and alignment easier. Robust collaborative leadership is critical to prevent silos.

A frequent weakness in under-designed investment functions is asset-class silos in which each specialist focuses on their asset class rather than the overall portfolio. In high-functioning offices, these domains may be governed separately but coordinated at the capital allocation level. That coordination is critical; without it, liquidity can be squeezed, risk can become concentrated and the total portfolio's flexibility can erode without anyone noticing. This alignment is often reinforced through governance design, ensuring that the investment committee and CIO see a single, consolidated picture of the portfolio and that performance is evaluated holistically.

3.6 Separating direct holdings from financial assets

One managing director described the 'logic tree' approach for families deciding how to deploy investable capital. It starts with a distinction between direct holdings (operating companies, controlling stakes or active entrepreneurial assets) and financial assets (liquid portfolios, fund commitments and marketable securities). Managing both under one team is possible but often suboptimal. The skills, networks, experience and management required differ.

Some solve this by establishing two distinct teams or entities, each with its own budget, leadership and key performance indicators. This avoids the cultural and operational confusion that can arise when a single team is stretched across both worlds.

A more flexible approach is to maintain generalist leadership at the top, supported by deal-specific expertise brought in as needed through entrepreneurs-in-residence, sector consultants or partnership arrangements. This ensures breadth of opportunity without locking into one niche.

Many families aspire to move beyond fund investing into direct deals, seeking greater control, engagement and potentially higher returns. The most effective way to do this is through a staged progression.

3.7 Building direct investment capability: a staged approach

Many families aspire to move beyond fund investing into direct deals, seeking greater control, engagement and potentially higher returns. The most effective way to do this is through a staged progression. Most begin with fund investments, which provide exposure, networks and learning without the operational burden of executing deals themselves. From there, families often add co-investments, allowing them to gain greater influence while still leaning on the GP's infrastructure and expertise. Only once the right team, governance and processes are firmly in place should a family develop full direct dealmaking capability. This phased build-up prevents overstretching too early and ensures that lessons are learned without risking disproportionate capital.

For families engaged in direct investing, access is everything. Relationships with GPs and co-investment networks determine the quality of deal flow. Large-cap private equity firms value family offices as co-investors because they can move quickly, commit flexibly and have patient capital. But access is not guaranteed. Relationships fade when GPs scale and families become less material. This is where mid-market and specialist managers can offer richer, more consistent opportunity sets. Families should think carefully about where they are genuinely wanted as capital partners and build their strategy around those relationships.

3.8 Integrating family priorities

Finally, the investment function must be integrated with the family's broader priorities. This includes aligning with legacy objectives, philanthropic commitments and next-generation engagement.

Some families purposefully invite younger family members to investment committee meetings, not to influence decisions, but to educate and prepare them for future roles. Some align part of the portfolio with values-based goals, such as ESG integration or impact investing, to reflect the family's public reputation and internal priorities.

The investment engine must be able to evolve. Next-generation members may have different priorities, investment styles and expectations for transparency. The best governance structures plan for this, gradually integrating new voices and perspectives without destabilising the process.

In the strongest family offices, the investment engine is an integrated, purpose-built function designed around the family's objectives, disciplined in execution and adaptable enough to remain effective as the family, markets and priorities change.

The use of independent advisers is one of the most underutilised and often misunderstood, tools in family office governance. When carefully chosen and properly embedded, they bring clarity, objectivity and healthy challenge to investment decision making.

4. Pillar III: The value of independent voices

The use of independent advisers is one of the most underutilised and often misunderstood, tools in family office governance. When carefully chosen and properly embedded, they bring clarity, objectivity and healthy challenge to investment decision making. They offer a safeguard against overconfidence, insularity and unchecked assumptions.

In the best family offices, independence is more than a box-ticking exercise; it is a conscious choice. Independent advisers bring an external perspective, are emotionally detached and are grounded in professional judgement. Yet in many offices, independent advisers are absent, underused or selected for the wrong reasons. The result is governance that may look good on paper but lacks real rigour in practice.

4.1 Defining true independence

True independent advisers who are part time have fewer financial conflicts. They have the freedom and obligation to challenge decisions, question assumptions and record dissent when necessary. This is much harder for the in-house team given that the ultimate decision maker is their paymaster.

Social ties, loyalties or longstanding business relationships can dilute the objectivity of independent advisers. An independent adviser is invaluable in their ability to speak truth to power and disagree constructively. Emotional distance is an asset: when markets turn or a pet project fails, independent advisers are more likely to separate the decision from the decision maker. That detachment allows for more honest post-mortems and more actionable learning. As one CIO put it: "The danger of having friends of the family on the investment committee is that no one wants to contradict them. Suddenly, everyone's nodding."

4.2 How independent advisers contribute

Independent advisers can serve in different roles depending on how the family office is structured, either as formal voting members of investment committees or as strategic advisers in a non-voting capacity. Both types of engagement can deliver meaningful value.

In decision-making committees, independent members contribute deep technical expertise and the discipline to test ideas rigorously under pressure. Advisory committees, meanwhile, benefit from broader perspectives: people think about wealth holistically, challenge groupthink and highlight strategic risks and opportunities that may sit outside the immediate investment lens. The most valuable advisers aren't always the loudest. They speak when it matters. That makes their voice land.

The most effective independent advisers help to clarify investment strategy, shape governance structures and embed a culture of disciplined, evidence-based decision making.

4.3 The amplifier effect

Independent advisers have a multiplier effect on the capabilities of both the CIO and the broader investment team. When properly selected and integrated, they amplify the CIO's effectiveness by validating recommendations and providing a credible second opinion when those recommendations face resistance. They improve decision quality by ensuring that key calls are stress-tested from multiple perspectives; and they serve as a kind of institutional memory, recalling lessons from both successes and failures.

Importantly, they also reinforce the professionalism of the office in the eyes of staff, partners and next-generation family members, helping to cultivate a culture where investment is treated with institutional rigour. Independent advisers are immune to internal politics and therefore their support, or challenge, carries particular weight. As one CIO put it: "The investment committee is not a constraint; it's a gift. It makes me better, protects me from blind spots and gives my decisions more weight with the family."

This multiplier effect is one reason independent advisers should be viewed not as a 'nice to have', but as a core element of investment best practice. Hired well, they do not dilute the family's influence but strengthen it by ensuring that influence is exercised with a broader perspective, meaningful challenge and long-term stewardship in mind.

4.4 Designing effective committees

Creating effective governance structures means choosing a variety of people not only with diverse perspectives and the right credentials, but also with the right mindset, temperament and cultural fit. Strong independent voices are confident without being combative. They ask hard questions without ego and engage constructively with the family's unique decision-making framework. As one seasoned investment committee chair explained: "Effective investment committees blend practitioners and generalists, with confidence to challenge but not be bruised if ignored."

Selection should follow a structured process, with clear criteria for expertise and cultural fit. Terms should be time bound to avoid stagnation and performance should be assessed like any other critical role. Several common pitfalls can undermine committee effectiveness.

One is the appointment of trusted friends or longstanding associates, favouring familiarity without considering sound governance principles. In practice, these relationships rarely produce genuine challenge.

Another is stale expertise: advisers whose knowledge has not kept pace with markets, leaving them unable to contribute meaningfully to complex or fast-moving decisions.

A third issue is homogeneity. When everyone around the table shares similar backgrounds or perspectives, discussions tend to result in polite agreement rather than meaningful debate. In each of these cases, the committee loses the very qualities that independence is meant to provide: objectivity, diversity of thought and disciplined oversight.

4.5 Overcoming principal resistance

Some principals resist outside voices, fearing a loss of control or unwelcome scrutiny. But independence, properly framed, provides a wealth of ideas and wisdom. It is not a threat, but a safeguard. It protects the principal's legacy by strengthening the rigour, transparency and defensibility of decisions.

It also sends a powerful cultural signal to staff, advisers and future generations that investment is treated as a serious discipline. Over time, this culture of openness, challenges and professionalism

In the strongest family offices, independence is not a last-minute add-on. It is built in from the start – a core design principle that strengthens strategy, deepens governance and can mitigate avoidable and significant errors.

becomes self-reinforcing. Debates deepen, documentation improves and the family office attracts higher-calibre professionals.

In the strongest family offices, independence is not a last-minute add-on. It is built in from the start – a core design principle that strengthens strategy, deepens governance and can mitigate avoidable and significant errors.

4.6 Embedding independence in governance

For independence to matter, it must be embedded and not symbolic. Independent members should receive the same information as other decision makers and their role, whether advisory or voting, must be clearly defined and respected.

Their contributions should be recorded and visible in the decision trail, reinforcing both accountability and transparency. And, most importantly, the family must be prepared to hear uncomfortable truths and engage in healthy debate to reach better decisions. Removing or sidelining an independent adviser for doing their job sends a clear message that challenge is welcome only when it is convenient, undermining the credibility of the entire governance structure.

Token independence, in fact, can be worse than none at all. Installing an 'independent' adviser who is a friend of the principal, avoids dissent or lacks relevant insight provides false reassurance and signals to others that the governance process is more form than substance.

5. Conclusion

Family office investment best practice combines financial capital with human capital.

First, the CIO is more than a technical expert. They are the steward of the investment process, balancing expertise with emotional intelligence in a deeply personal environment. Second, the investment function must be intentionally designed, lean where it can be and rigorous where it must be, always aligned to the family's objectives, scale and culture. Third, independent voices are not decorative; they are a multiplier of capability, bringing distance, discipline and perspective that can protect both the portfolio and the family.

Families with effective family offices are more holistic in their approach. They embrace governance not as bureaucracy, but as a protective cocoon. They hire CIOs whose expertise and judgement they trust and give them the mandate and resources to succeed. They design investment engines around their true needs, not institutional templates.

They also recognise that none of this is static. Governance, team structure and priorities must evolve as markets shift and their family grows. The discipline lies in keeping the core principles intact; aligning purpose, clarity of responsibilities and accountability; and ensuring that all values are voiced and considered.

Families that invest intentionally in the people, processes and governance that shape decisions are best equipped to protect their wealth and their freedom to pursue what matters most. In the end, the architecture of the portfolio is only as good as the architecture of decision making.

VIII. Preserving the family voice: legal insights into governance and generational wealth

Suzanne Johnston
Stephenson Harwood LLP

1. How family constitutions are shaping legacies with wit, warmth and vision

1.1 Introduction

My family life is noisy: two young children, a husband and multiple pets. It is louder still when we introduce grandparents, siblings and cousins into the mix! Often my voice is drowned out by the sound of playing, squabbles and, if I am lucky, laughter. The intergenerational high-net-worth families that I work with in Asia are no different.

When it comes to working with families, it is critical that, as advisers, we amplify their voices not only during our conversations, but also in the documents that we craft together. One such document is the family constitution, which has become increasingly important for families that seek to nurture, beyond financial success, shared values, a sense of belonging and, often, a meaningful role for family members in the family business.

It is thought that the modern-day family constitution has its roots in the medieval concept of 'house laws' of royal families in Europe. House laws aimed to preserve family power and wealth by establishing rules on succession, inheritance, leadership and position. In a similar way, family constitutions today are utilised to provide an organised and personal framework to support the preservation of the family's legacy, vision and wealth over time. However, they are no longer just for royalty ...

1.2 The role of the family business lawyer: champion of the family's own voice

Lawyers such as I have often been called 'private wealth lawyers', but that term does not completely reflect what we do. A more appropriate designation might be 'family business lawyer', as this title accurately represents my advisory role with entrepreneurs and acknowledges the integral connection between business planning and succession planning.

A family business lawyer must be an expert listener who engages with the telling of the family's story. It is imperative to resist dominating discussions or drafting based on assumptions or personal views (and yes, sometimes this can be incredibly challenging when the outlook is so alien to my own). It is my honour and responsibility to create space for the family's voice to emerge in the documents that I help draft.

The best constitutions are crafted through open dialogue, with me acting as a facilitator –ensuring that all perspectives are heard and that the final document truly reflects the family's aspirations, values and traditions.

My role includes:

- facilitating inclusive discussions, encouraging contributions from all generations;
- helping the family to articulate their values, goals and priorities;
- ensuring that the language of the constitution is authentic and accessible – it needs to sound like the family;
- advising on the interaction between the constitution and legally binding documents and ensuring that the documents are harmonised;
- navigating cross-jurisdictional considerations and how to compromise and prioritise competing factors;
- designing practical, imaginative and workable dispute resolution mechanisms that don't feel too rigid or intimidating; and
- encouraging the family to think about how decisions should be taken and when.

I see myself as a guide, a sounding board and arbiter in cases where families are finding it difficult to agree on the best way forward. I am not there to 'tell' the family what to do – my role is to let them know what is possible.

Drafting a family constitution is a rare opportunity for honest conversation and reflection between family members. It's a chance to bring together voices from different generations, to acknowledge both the family's proudest moments and the lessons learned along the way.

2. Beginnings: where to start when drafting a family constitution

2.1 It's good to talk (and listen)

For many families, their legacy is shaped by tradition – stories of their ancestors and informal understandings as to how 'things are done'. As an adviser, I relish the opportunity to hear the stories of the families that I work with – not only because they are often fascinating from a historical perspective (I am a history graduate and partial to a good family tree tale), but also because their stories are critical to the formation of an effective family constitution and governance framework.

The informal understandings that are historically passed on by guidance from elder family members and via stories are vital to designing a more structured approach to family governance utilising the family constitution. It is now a necessity for many families to formally enshrine their ethos, values and how they interact in a centralised document, as they have grown more complex and geographically dispersed. However, at their core, families are shaped by their informal understandings and interactions; this should not be lost in the process of formalising values via documentation. Put simply, the family constitution must 'sound' like the family.

Drafting a family constitution is a rare opportunity for honest conversation and reflection between family members. It's a chance to bring together voices from different generations, to acknowledge both the family's proudest moments and the lessons learned along the way. In doing so, families can build a document that is genuinely theirs, filled with purpose and designed to strengthen connections well into the future. To achieve this, advisers need to listen and resist the urge to impose their own views on how a family constitution should look or read. A family constitution isn't legally binding – and nor should it be. It is a living document that must be capable of evolution over the passage of time.

2.2 Why have a family constitution?

I am often asked: "What's the point of a family constitution? Do I really need one?" The answer is: it depends. While a family constitution isn't right or necessary for every family, it can play several key roles in guiding a family's journey and, at the very least, warrants consideration.

2.3 Key 'ingredients' of a family constitution

- ***Values and vision:*** What does the family stand for? What are its hopes and aspirations for the future? What might stand in the way of these?
- ***Governance structures:*** Who makes decisions and how? Is there a family council, a family assembly or just a WhatsApp group that pings every five minutes?
- ***Succession planning:*** How will leadership, sensibility and ownership pass from one generation to the next? How do we ensure that family members feel valued for their own skills, talents and personalities?
- ***Dispute resolution:*** What happens when disagreements arise? Clients regularly tell me that their family doesn't argue and that's great. But we need to face facts – disputes happen and it's best to resolve them quickly and amicably.
- ***Communication protocols:*** How does the family share information, make announcements and avoid overcommunication (especially now that we are inundated with modes of communication)? It has become increasingly challenging to find communication methods that work for multiple generations.

3. An in-depth examination of the family constitution and its applications

3.1 Succession planning

The most crucial role of the family constitution is in succession planning. Succession of wealth and business leadership is, without a doubt, one of the most sensitive issues that a family will face. In Asia, the families that I work with are often also concerned with succession of responsibility within the family – for example, who will take care of mum and dad into old age and how vulnerable or younger family members should be nurtured and protected.

Regarding wealth devolution, the constitution plays a role by specifying how various family planning arrangements interrelate. For example, a family may have a singular family trust or multiple family trusts, alongside wills for each family member. A matriarch may decide to support one child through her will and another through a trust. The rationale for this approach could be tax or age driven, or a combination of varying factors. Without communicating the rationale and explaining how this will work in practice, there can be tensions between siblings as to their differing treatment. A family constitution and the discussions that shape it help to mitigate the risk of misunderstanding (and rendering useless) the legally binding planning that a family has implemented.

The family constitution is also utilised to assign roles to family members in the family business or within a trust structure. For example, I have worked with families that have deployed the family constitution to set out criteria for branches of the family to be eligible to sit on protector committees or investment committees for their family trusts. In this way, the eligibility requirements for the adoption of such roles can be spelled out so that family members have clear expectations and benchmarks to work towards.

Similarly, another family that I worked with harnessed the family constitution to detail how family members with different roles within the family business would receive distributions from the family trusts. The quantum, regularity and timing of the distribution were dependent on their role, seniority and tenure within the family business.

In this way, the family constitution can be used to provide direction, remove uncertainty and set clear expectations in relation to the sharing of family wealth.

3.2 Business continuity

In my experience, family enterprises thrive when there are clear protocols for decision making, participation and inclusion.

It is common for families to outline in the constitution their vision for the future of the family business or businesses. This may include guidance as to when a business may be sold (ie, at what size or price, and whom to consult) or wound up and its assets dispersed (particularly common in the context of property businesses). Alternatively, the focus may be on how the family business can be sustained into the future via diversification or investment in new technologies and renewables.

I have worked with families that have successfully harnessed the constitution to set out distinct roles for family members in the family business, provided that they have attained certain milestones. These could include holding a bachelor's degree, meeting age requirements, having proven personal investment experience, contributing to the family and maintaining good conduct.

Increasingly, the families that I work with understand that not every family member wants to, or can, participate directly in the family business. Recognising this is as important as finding roles for family members in the business. The families that get the most out of their family constitutions understand that we all have different gifts, talents and goals. Whereas one child may express enthusiasm for participating in the family business, another might view the prospect with apprehension or prefer to pursue an alternative career path.

Part of my job is to give family members a voice so that they can describe how they see themselves fitting into the future. The outcomes can be surprising. A family member who may think they have nothing to contribute to the business because they are not 'business minded' can find themselves in a critical role nonetheless as lead HR or in business relations. In another case I worked on, it was agreed that one of the siblings would have no role in the family business but would have a key role on the family council and would be chief organiser of annual family gatherings and holidays.

As a living document, the constitution serves to help the family business adapt while staying true to the family's core values and embracing different family members' talents. It is, in essence, an expression of the family as a whole and its members' different strengths and weaknesses. It is, above all, a tool of inclusion and belonging.

3.3 Dispute resolution

One of the most critical roles of the family constitution is to clarify how families should hear and resolve disputes. All families argue and some family members shout louder than others. It is essential, therefore to have agreed dispute resolution procedures in place to preserve family harmony and reduce the risk of undermining the family's hard work in designing the family constitution and the legal documentation surrounding it – not to mention to avoid the escalating legal fees that can arise from disputes that are not resolved swiftly and fairly.

All families argue and some family members shout louder than others. It is essential, therefore, to have agreed dispute resolution procedures in place to preserve family harmony.

When it comes to dispute resolution procedures, it is important to build in layers of potential resolution processes. Usually, the initial approach involves a 'soft' resolution, such as arranging a meeting between the disputing parties – sometimes including other family members – to openly discuss the issue. Afterwards, the family might hold a vote and consult the family council; if things get more serious, they could arrange a meeting with an outside mediator. As a last resort, dispute resolution procedures may set out how to engage with legal counsel, including who should bear the costs of this.

3.4 Disputes and disagreements

Acknowledging that disputes and disagreements can and do happen – and implementing planning to manage them – is critical to the success of the family. So, what do I recommend?

- ***Clear procedures:*** By setting out agreed steps for resolving disputes – whether it's a heart to heart over coffee or a formal mediation process – the constitution helps to de-escalate tempers.
- ***Neutral ground:*** Having the family council or assembly as the first arbiter in disagreements can help to provide a fair and free way of managing disputes. This is one of the core reasons why clear guidance as to eligibility for membership and election to

the family council matters. It must be respected as a fair, neutral and representative body.

- ***Mediation and arbitration:*** Despite best efforts, the family may not agree. The constitution may provide for mediation with a neutral third party or even arbitration for binding decisions.
- ***Expert determination:*** For technical disputes – say, about business valuations or investment strategy – the constitution can call in an independent expert. This avoids the urge to rely on ChatGPT for answers.
- ***Voting mechanisms:*** As emotional decision making can lead to disputes, having clear voting protocols in place can help to mitigate the risk of this. Sometimes, democracy is the best policy. Constitutions may allow for majority or supermajority votes, ensuring that decisions reflect the will of the family, not just the loudest voice.

3.5 The importance of humour and empathy in family governance

We have discussed the more traditional ingredients that we would expect to find in the family constitution. However, it is important to understand that humour and empathy also have a place.

Family meetings should be fun and engaging. Some of my families choose to host them while taking an annual family holiday to an exotic destination or over dinner in a private room. It is important to foster a

Family meetings should be fun and engaging. Some of my families choose to host them while taking an annual family holiday to an exotic destination or over dinner in a private room. It is important to foster a sense of belonging and a feeling that family members are on the same team.

sense of belonging and a feeling that family members are on the same team. I encourage my families to bring a little joy into their discussions and not to get bogged down in the seriousness of the conversation.

Empathy is vital. It allows family members to see things from each other's perspectives, to listen as well as speak and to find common ground even when opinions diverge. A constitution can encourage empathy through allowing for opportunities that promote open dialogue, active listening and respect for different viewpoints.

4. Good governance

So, now that we understand the uses of the family constitution, what does good governance in a family constitution look like?

4.1 Governance structures: family councils, assemblies, Zoom calls and WhatsApp

In a world where there are increasing modes of communication and different generations have varying comfort levels, it's becoming harder for families to find a common means to talk. That's why having a family constitution that can act as a roadmap for how families can organise themselves, make decisions and, crucially, communicate even when the WiFi cuts out (or grandad can't use Zoom) is becoming even more valuable.

4.2 Types of governance bodies

Getting the structure right matters and different forums represent an opportunity to shape conversations in unique ways. The nature of a conversation over the dinner table is different by necessity from discussions during a family assembly and family council meeting. Similarly, a family assembly and family council allow for less formal interactions than the board of a company. In a formal setting, there is often a need for quick, decisive and determinative action, which leaves little room for listening and understanding. In contrast, a more informal setting can offer a fluid agenda, facilitating open conversations where a determinative answer does not need to be reached immediately.

The most common governance bodies are as follows.

(a) Family assembly

The 'town hall' of the family, open to all family members (although note that different families define 'family' in different ways). Assemblies are usually held annually or biannually and serve as a forum for major decisions, information sharing and, occasionally, the airing of grievances. The family assembly:

- approves major decisions (eg, changes to the constitution or significant investments or sale of the family business);

- provides a forum for all voices to be heard;
- elects or appoints members to the family council or committees; and
- brings the family together.

(b) Family council

I compare this to the family's board of directors, often comprising a smaller group of family members representing different branches, generations or businesses. The family council meets regularly to discuss strategy, resolve issues, approve decisions and make recommendations. Its functions include:

- setting the agenda for family meetings;
- facilitating communication between family members and the business;
- overseeing implementation of the family constitution;
- addressing disputes and making recommendations on key issues; and
- representing multiple generations of the family.

(c) Advisory boards and committees

I have seen some families create specialised committees, particularly where a trust structure is in operation. These can include an investment, protector, philanthropic or education committee. The main responsibilities of advisory boards and committees are to:

- focus on specific areas (eg, investments, philanthropy, education, use of technology/visibility);
- report back to the counsel or assembly with recommendations;
- include family members with specific skill sets;
- provide an opportunity for the younger generation to have a voice; and
- represent different interests and passions within the family.

(d) Harnessing technology

Inclusion matters, so in facilitating the meetings of family committees it is critical to find a medium that works for all. It is important for families to agree upfront whether they are comfortable communicating virtually and if so, via what medium (eg, Zoom, Teams, WhatsApp or WeChat). Some individuals may prefer not to participate in virtual meetings; therefore, families may stipulate that certain crucial decisions – such as those involving the sale of a family business – must be discussed during an in-person meeting.

4.3 Roles and responsibilities

If it isn't already clear from the above, in my view, identifiable and understandable roles and responsibilities that make room for different

Some individuals may prefer not to participate in virtual meetings; therefore, families may stipulate that certain crucial decisions – such as those involving the sale of a family business – must be discussed during an in-person meeting.

family members and generations are the backbone of effective family governance. Without them, meetings can quickly descend into chaos or become pointless (we have all been on a Zoom call where we've asked ourselves: "Is this a good use of my time?").

It is important to appoint a chairperson or secretary to each committee to ensure that meetings are productive and decisions are recorded. This person can be responsible for ensuring that a quorum for decision making is present and that anyone who can't attend has had an opportunity in advance to share their views on the topic at hand. However, families need to choose their chairperson carefully. Dominant chairs don't always manage to hear all the voices. A suitable candidate will be firm yet fair, with the ability to facilitate discussion unantagonistically.

4.4 Succession planning for leadership and membership

The family constitution should set out clear procedures for how leadership roles are transferred from one generation to the next, managing expectations and minimising drama.

4.5 Transparent criteria (don't keep moving the goalposts)

Define the qualifications, experience or training required for leadership roles – for example, formal education, work experience or a proven ability to survive three consecutive family meetings without raising their voice! Don't forget, personality matters and it is important that the right group of family members be brought together to staff a particular committee.

4.6 Mentorship, training and staggered transitions

Encourage outgoing leaders to mentor their successors, sharing not just knowledge but also the unwritten rules and family lore that keep the wheels turning. If you wish, you can formally enshrine a handover procedure in the constitution or have committee members appoint their own successors to shadow them for a fixed period of time before they step down (eg, three years).

4.7 Regular review

Build in regular reviews of leadership roles and succession plans, adapting as the family grows and changes. As families expand and the connections between relatives become more distant, disagreements among family members often become more common.

5. Legal enforceability

5.1 Family constitutions are not legally binding ... or are they?

Generally, family constitutions are not intended to be legally binding and that's okay. There are other legally binding documents that

Significantly, if a family dispute escalates to court, the family constitution could be submitted as evidence of the family's intentions. Just because a family constitution isn't legally binding doesn't mean it can't have future legal effects or serve as persuasive evidence in court.

encircle them. But just because they are generally not legally binding does not render them legally insignificant. In short, family constitutions can have legal implications.

5.2 Legal implications

A family constitution acts as a factual record, an affirmation of family commitment and a guide for contractual implementation, as well as a supplemental layer of governance of the family business. It is intended as a consensus-creating device. Unlike legal acts, legal facts do not give rise to enforceable obligations by themselves. However, they may become legally significant in the context of the broader legal relationships surrounding the family constitution.

Significantly, if a family dispute escalates to court, the family constitution could be submitted as evidence of the family's intentions. Just because a family constitution isn't legally binding doesn't mean it can't have future legal effects or serve as persuasive evidence in court. As such, it is critical to seek legal advice in formulating its terms and to ensure that family members fully understand its purview. Remember, if the family constitution is not intended to be legally binding, its provisions should reflect this.

To exclude or ignore the indirect legal effects of the family constitution undermines its importance and significance.

5.3 Shareholders' agreements are not family constitutions

In relation to the family business, family constitutions should not be confused with shareholders' agreements. Shareholders' agreements are normally legally binding. Some family members who are not shareholders – for instance, beneficiaries of a family trust which owns shares in the business – might be a party to the constitution. Similarly, there may be shareholders, such as external investors, who are not party to the family constitution but are party to the shareholders' agreement. The biggest difference is that a family constitution often deals with issues that are incapable of being the basis of a binding legal agreement.

In my view, it is dangerous to conflate the shareholders' agreement and the family constitution, even if they have some overlap in content. From a legal point of view, it might be tempting to draft family constitutions as binding shareholders' agreements. However, focusing on legal ownership can reduce the benefits of strategic planning that are offered via the family constitution. Both documents are helpful when designed to complement each other.

5.4 Legal enforceability across jurisdictions

The legal enforceability of family constitutions varies significantly across jurisdictions. In many common law countries (eg, England and Wales, Australia, Canada and the United States), family constitutions are considered non-binding unless they meet the requirements for a contract – that is, offer, acceptance, consideration and a clear intention to create legal relations. Rather, family constitutions are often construed as moral or aspirational commitments rather than legal obligations.

It is well-established case law in common law jurisdictions that enforceable contracts must involve consideration. In the family context, it has long been accepted that domestic agreements – for example, between husband and wife – are not intended to be legally binding (*Balfour v Balfour* [1919] 2 KB 571).

Civil law jurisdictions (eg, in Europe, Japan and parts of Asia) may take a different view. In these countries, family constitutions may be recognised as binding if they comply with certain statutory requirements. Still, their primary influence is rooted in the moral and social sphere rather than the legal one.

6. The generational perspective: "Mum, I'm bored!"

The families with whom I work are expressing growing concerns regarding the next generation and are seeking effective strategies to involve and safeguard them. We are entering an era in which artificial intelligence will substantially influence future employment opportunities and social interactions for the next generation. The future, as ever, is unknown and uncertain.

The challenge for any family constitution is not just to preserve wealth and values, but to do so in a way that keeps the family flame burning brightly – in the face of future change and challenges.

6.1 Engaging the next generation

As parents, we know that our time with our children is finite. That's why it is important to ensure that our interactions with our children are meaningful and engaging. This can be difficult to achieve when trying to involve younger family members, from teenagers onwards in family governance. However, engaging the next generation is essential if the family's legacy is to endure. A family constitution can be a powerful tool for inclusion, provided that it's wielded with a bit of creativity, thoughtfulness and patience.

6.2 My top tips for involving the next generation

- ***Early involvement:*** Ask younger family members to observe or participate in family meetings, even if their initial contributions are limited. They need not stay for the entire meeting.
- ***Voice and vote:*** Give the next generation a real say – perhaps a

We are entering an era in which artificial intelligence will substantially influence future employment opportunities and social interactions for the next generation. The future, as ever, is unknown and uncertain.

vote on certain issues or a seat or shadowing role on the family council. For a family constitution to remain sustainable, it is essential that the perspectives of the next generation are included.

- ***Projects and initiatives:*** Encourage the younger generation to lead family projects, philanthropic initiatives, sustainability or innovation committees – harness what they are interested in and good at. This not only builds skills but also fosters a sense of ownership and pride in the family enterprise.
- ***Education, mentorship and the family 'apprenticeship':*** A family constitution shouldn't be perceived as a set of archaic rules to bind future generations. Instead, it is a roadmap for developing future leaders. Education and mentorship are the cornerstones of this journey. The older generation has a responsibility to nurture and encourage the next generation.
- ***Formal education:*** Many families include provisions (financial or otherwise) for supporting the next generation's education, whether through scholarships, internships or additional tutoring to cater for special needs.
- ***Mentorship:*** Pairing younger family members with experienced mentors (inside or outside the family) helps to transfer not just knowledge, but wisdom. I regularly have client's children as interns in my team – they gain valuable insights into why their family is engaging with a lawyer in the first place and get to see how other families plan for wealth devolution.

- ***Family apprenticeship:*** Some constitutions set out structured 'apprenticeships', allowing the next generation to rotate through different roles in the family business or philanthropic activities.

7. A change will do you good

7.1 Adapting the constitution as the family evolves

Families evolve – new members are born, others marry in (or divorce out) and some pass on. This is why the family constitution must be a living document capable of changing. The family's views will evolve over time, as will their voice. Just a decade ago, most of the clients I worked with excluded adopted children from benefiting from family wealth. Now, with the proliferation of assisted pregnancies, including via surrogacy, most of my clients agree that children born via surrogacy and adopted children should be included as beneficiaries.

The family constitution should allow for regular reviews – generally every few years or if a major event occurs, such as the death of a matriarch or patriarch. This ensures that the document stays relevant, reflecting the family's current reality. It is important that the routes to amending the constitution are made clear and that they are fair. Voting on changes should be transparent. A particular challenge is ensuring that family members can give feedback on any proposed amendments to the family constitution. The best constitutions are those that listen as well as they speak. So, it is important to set out a consultation period for key changes/decisions during which all family members can have a say and feel heard.

8. Conclusion

8.1 Best practices and recommendations

- Include all generations in the drafting process to foster engagement and relevance.
- Update the constitution regularly to reflect changes in the family or its enterprises.
- Clearly distinguish between moral guidelines and aspirations and legally enforceable provisions.
- Use supporting legal documents for important matters such as succession and asset distribution where there are legal formalities that must be complied with.
- Promote open communication, transparency and education about the constitution's purpose.
- Remain flexible – the family constitution may look very different by the time it is drafted from what you originally intended.

8.2 A final word

A family constitution is so much more than a document. It's a living embodiment of a family's values, aspirations and collective wisdom – a blueprint, but not a permanent mark, for preserving the family voice across generations.

We need to be realistic; it will not prevent every disagreement or guarantee harmony in perpetuity. But it will provide an agreed framework that can be used to navigate challenges. The process of creating the family constitution is very beneficial to the family in and of itself, as to arrive at a workable framework, the family must hold open and revealing discussions. As a historical record, family constitutions are powerful and insightful windows into a family's identity, values and world outlooks. Yes, their legal force is limited, but that is not to be viewed in the negative. While legal documents are common and easily obtained, a family constitution offers unmatched significance by helping to create a unified family story, fostering cooperation and supporting families as they navigate transitions across generations.

When crafted with the family at the heart, with inclusiveness and thoughtfulness, a family constitution becomes a living document – one that adapts, unites and inspires. The enduring value of a family constitution lies in its ability to evolve alongside the family it serves. It's not a set of handcuffs or a life sentence; it's a document that can and must be malleable over time.

The true wealth of a family is measured not just in assets, but in relationships, shared purpose and the stories that bind generations. So, as your family gather – around the dinner table, the boardroom or, if they are anything like my family, the TV for a movie – remember, the collective family voice is precious. A family constitution allows you to preserve that voice with a sprinkle of wit, warmth and vision to breathe life into what really matters: the financial and emotional wellbeing of the family.

About the authors

Greg B Davies
Head of behavioural finance, Oxford Risk
greg.davies@oxfordrisk.com

Greg B Davies is a leading expert in behavioural finance and decision making under risk and uncertainty. He is head of behavioural finance at Oxford Risk, where he works with wealth managers, family offices and financial institutions globally to design tools and frameworks that help individuals and families to make better long-term financial decisions.

Greg holds a PhD in behavioural decision theory from the University of Cambridge and is the author of *Behavioural Investment Management: An Efficient Alternative to Modern Portfolio Theory* (McGraw-Hill). His work focuses on how emotional comfort, individual financial personality and group dynamics shape real-world decision making – particularly in complex contexts such as inheritance, succession and long-term investing.

Previously, Greg was a managing director at Barclays Wealth, where in 2006 he founded the banking industry's first dedicated behavioural finance team. His career has consistently bridged academic research and practical application, with a particular emphasis on designing decision processes that work for real people rather than theoretical models.

Jennifer East
Founder, ONIDA Family Advisors
jennifer@onida.ca

Jennifer East has spent two decades helping global family enterprises and family offices to navigate the opportunities and complexities of multi-generational wealth. Her work focuses on helping families to clarify purpose and wealth identity, navigate succession, strengthen family dynamics and develop rising-generation leaders. She also supports families in creating governance structures that reinforce continuity and shared stewardship across generations.

Drawing on her lived experience as a next-generation family business leader and entrepreneur, Jennifer also serves – with her husband – as co-chair of Class Afloat, a mission-driven school at sea with a 40-year legacy of experiential education. This combination of advisory and family business leadership gives her rare insight into the realities of multi-generational family life and next-gen development.

A trained executive coach, facilitator and mediator, Jennifer is a fellow of the Family Firm Institute (FFI) and holds FFI's Advanced Certificate in Family Business Advising. For more than a decade, she has been a highly rated instructor in FFI's Global Education Network and a sought-after speaker at international family enterprise and family office forums.

Sonya Gladstone
Associate, RAH Partners
sonya.gladstone@rahpartners.com

Sonya Gladstone is an associate at RAH Partners, supporting clients in leadership advisory and family business consulting. With a background in psychology and a deep interest in human behaviour, she is motivated by bringing individuals and teams together to enhance performance and achieve their goals. A graduate of Yale University with a degree in psychology focused on team and organisational dynamics, Sonya's academic work has explored group behaviour and interpersonal relationships, shaping her interest in business and management psychology.

Beyond her professional experience, she has been involved in elite rowing for many years. As coxswain for the Leander Club Men's Senior Team and previously for Yale's Division I Men's Heavyweight Crew, she contributed to several championship seasons. This experience strengthened her leadership, communication and composure under pressure – qualities that she brings to her work at RAH Partners.

Rhian-Anwen Hamill
Senior adviser and coach, RAH Partners;
Director of family enterprise, Institute of Entrepreneurship and Private Capital, London Business School
rhian-anwen.hamill@rahpartners.com

Rhian-Anwen Hamill is a senior adviser to global families, an executive coach and director of family enterprise at the Institute of Entrepreneurship and Private Capital at London Business School. With over 25 years of experience in governance, succession planning, talent and next-generation preparation, she works with family collectives, FTSE companies and privately held businesses. Her expertise spans business, coaching, psychology, philanthropy and the arts.

Beginning her career at Goldman Sachs, Rhian has spent more than three decades in financial and professional services and, since 2005, has led her own advisory and coaching firm, RAH Partners. She has also served at board and C-suite level in several charities.

Educated at United World College of the Atlantic, Cambridge University and internationally recognised institutes in leadership and psychology, Rhian also serves on the council of the Hay Festival.

James Hann
Partner, Digitalis
james.hann@digitalis.com

James Hann is a partner at Digitalis and a specialist in the integration of digital intelligence and online reputation management. He provides clients with guidance on complex online matters and open-source intelligence support and helps to develop pre-emptive strategies to manage clients' reputations. He supports communications and law firms, public and private companies, and governments. Before joining Digitalis, James spent eight years in the military, serving on multiple operations across the Middle East and North Africa.

Suzanne Johnston
Partner, head of private wealth, Singapore, Stephenson Harwood LLP
suzanne.johnston@stephensonharwood.com

Suzanne Johnston is a top-tier private wealth lawyer with over 12 years' experience in Singapore and the founder of Stephenson Harwood's private wealth practice in the region. Renowned for her rare UK tax expertise in Asia-Pacific and deep knowledge of trust, succession and estate planning, she advises clients with complex, cross-border assets. Suzanne is highly client focused, offering practical, jargon-free guidance to individuals, families and institutions.

on wills, trusts, family offices and regulatory challenges. She is committed to building long-term relationships and ensuring that clients feel supported through complex legal landscapes. Within the firm, Suzanne champions female career progression and mental health, and was instrumental in developing policies for infertility and baby loss. She is ranked as a Leading Partner in *The Legal 500* and listed among the top 100 lawyers in Singapore by the *Asia Business Law Journal.*

Samuel Lawson
Relationship manager, Acorn Capital Advisers
samuel.lawson@acorncapitaladvisers.com

Samuel Lawson is a dedicated and detail-oriented professional with a solid foundation in investment management, client relations and operational efficiency. Previously an account manager at Sydney-based private wealth firm Statton Partners, he specialises in business optimisation with a client-focused approach, delivering bespoke, transparent and effective financial solutions through personalised service.

Sam holds a bachelor's degree in political economics and Mandarin from the University of Sydney.

Jessica McGawley
Founder, Dallington
jessica@dallingtonassociates.com

Jessica McGawley is a psychological consultant, mediator and the founder of Dallington. For over 17 years, she has worked with more than 150 ultra-high-net-worth families, advising on the relational and psychological complexities associated with significant wealth.

Her work focuses on supporting families as they navigate the often private and challenging realities of adolescence, inheritance, succession and identity development in the context of wealth and public success. Jessica's particular expertise lies in intergenerational relationships, conflict resolution and the impact of significant wealth on individuals and family systems.

She frequently collaborates with legal, financial and fiduciary professionals to ensure that technical and governance structures are underpinned by resilient human dynamics. In addition to her advisory practice, Jessica contributes thought leadership on family dynamics and wealth psychology and is a trusted facilitator of family meetings and next-generation development programmes.

She holds an undergraduate degree in ethnomusicology and African culture from SOAS, a postgraduate diploma in counselling and psychotherapy and a master's degree in consulting psychology from The Tavistock and Portman NHS Foundation. She is also a qualified mediator.

Alongside her professional work, she runs an annual scholarship programme supporting students who require additional psychological and educational support.

Maya Prabhu
Managing director, J.P. Morgan Private Bank
maya.am.prabhu@jpmorgan.com

Maya Prabhu leads a team of client advisers in the United Kingdom dedicated to helping clients define their wealth purpose and achieve their goals. Her team offers comprehensive support, from thought leadership and wealth planning to banking, investing, lending, philanthropy and family governance.

With nearly two decades of experience as a trusted adviser to wealthy individuals and families across the United Kingdom, Europe the Middle East and Asia, she brings deep expertise in family governance (processes for developing culture, teamwork and communication), next-generation engagement, family office creation and rewarding philanthropy strategies.

Maya holds practising certificates in family business advising and family wealth advising from the Family Firm Institute (Boston, USA) and a certificate in executive coaching from the Henley Business School (University of Reading), and is an accredited mediator from Regents University. She is a member of the teaching faculty for the Family Firm Institute's GEN courses and for the Society of Trust and Estate Practitioners' diploma certificate in private client advising. Maya serves as an independent member of the governing council of the University of Warwick and is a member of the advisory board at Warwick Business School.

Colby Richardson
Managing director, Blue Forge Capital
colby@blueforgecap.com

Colby Richardson is the managing director of Blue Forge Capital, a Canadian investment platform that backs early-stage venture funds and technology companies across Canada, the United States and the United Kingdom. His work focuses on identifying and supporting emerging fund managers building in fintech, AI and deep tech. Colby currently serves as a director on the board of Richardson Financial Group. Prior to founding Blue Forge, he supported corporate development for growth-stage start-ups. Colby holds an MBA from London Business School and a BA from Brown University. He also holds the ICD.D designation through the Institute of Corporate Directors.

Samuel Shaw
Client relationship manager, Acorn Capital Advisers
samuel.shaw@acorncapitaladvisers.com

Samuel Shaw provides support to clients and the team by overseeing investment reporting, bespoke projects and communication with external service providers. He previously worked at an independent financial adviser in Malta, where he was a relationship manager in the client services team working with clients globally.

He was chairman and treasurer of Papplewick Young Farmers' Club, where he led fundraising initiatives for both the club and charitable organisations – most notably the Nottinghamshire and Lincolnshire Air Ambulance.

Samuel holds an LLB in law with legal studies in Europe from the University of Reading and spent one year at Uppsala University in Sweden. He has obtained the Investment Management Certificate.

Sally Tennant
Founder, Acorn Capital Advisers
sally.tennant@acorncapitaladvisers.com

Sally Tennant OBE has many years of investment, banking and management experience as an investment manager and chief executive. From 2011 to 2014, she was chief executive of Kleinwort Benson. She was previously chief executive of Lombard Odier (UK) Ltd and chief executive of Schroders Private Banking.

Sally is a non-executive director of B-FLEXION Group Holdings SA and Younited Financial SA, a leading European consumer credit business. She also sits on the investment committees and boards for a number of Acorn Capital Advisers' clients.

She is a trustee and chairs the Investment Committee for the Royal Academy Trust. She is also a patron of Tommy's, the baby charity.

Sally holds a degree in politics from the University of Durham.

About Globe Law and Business

Globe Law and Business was established in 2005. From the very beginning, we set out to create legal books that are sufficiently high level to be of real use to the experienced professional, yet still accessible and easy to navigate. Most of our authors are drawn from Magic Circle and other top commercial firms, both in the United Kingdom and internationally.

Our titles are carefully produced, with the utmost attention paid to editorial, design and production processes. We hope this results in high-quality publications that are easy to read and a pleasure to own.

In 2021, we were very pleased to announce the start of a new chapter for Globe Law and Business following the acquisition of law books under the imprint Ark Publishing. Our law firm management list is now significantly expanded with many well-known and loved Ark Publishing titles.

We have also launched an online content platform, Globe Law Online, which allows for easy access across firms. Details of all titles included can be found at www.globelawonline.com. Email glo@globelawandbusiness.com for further details and to arrange a free trial for you or your firm.

We'd very much like to hear from you with your thoughts and ideas for improving what we offer. Please do feel free to email me at sian@globelawandbusiness.com. Happy reading and thank you for your time.

Sian O'Neill
Managing director
Globe Law and Business
www.globelawandbusiness.com